Find Your Blindspot in the Classroom

Find Your Blindspot in the Classroom offers both an alternative and a complement to standard professional development, instructional coaching, and teacher evaluation. Author Anne Bonnycastle reveals 10 common blindspots that can be challenging for teachers, whether you are in year one or 20. She provides practical strategies to help you find your own blindspot and then shows how you can improve that area by incorporating a professional practice focus.

The book's unique, no-frills, personalized approach will help you improve your classroom instruction, focusing on the effect that your teaching has on students. The research-supported strategies will help you increase your effectiveness, regardless of the supports available within your school.

Whether you have a mentor or coach guiding you or are using the book on your own, this book will be your trusty guide as you grow on your journey as an educator.

Dr. Anne Bonnycastle has been a teacher, administrator, department head, and instructional coach in both public and independent schools in British Columbia since 1996. Professional development has been her career-long focus: attending it, delivering it, researching about it. This book culminates a decade of working to understand teacher development.

Anne has an MA in educational psychology and a Doctoral degree in Music Education and was a recipient of the Distinguished Teacher Award, 2019 U.S. Presidential Scholars' Program.

T0386510

Also Available from Routledge Eye On Education

(www.routledge.com/K-12)

Easy and Effective Professional Development: The Power of Peer Observation to Improve Teaching
Catherine Beck, Paul D'Elia, Michael W. Lamond

101 Answers for New Teachers and Their Mentors, 4th Edition: Effective Teaching Tips for Daily Classroom Use
Annette Breaux

What Great Teachers Do Differently, 3rd Edition: Nineteen Things That Matter Most
Todd Whitaker

Classroom Management from the Ground Up
Todd Whitaker, Katherine Whitaker, Madeline Whitaker Good

The Meditation and Mindfulness Edge: Becoming a Sharper, Healthier, and Happier Teacher
Lisa Klein

Embracing Adult SEL: An Educator's Guide to Personal Social Emotional Learning Success
Wendy Turner

Find Your Blindspot in the Classroom

Improving Your Effectiveness as a Teacher

Anne Bonnycastle

Routledge
Taylor & Francis Group
NEW YORK AND LONDON

First published 2025
by Routledge
605 Third Avenue, New York, NY 10158

and by Routledge
4 Park Square, Milton Park, Abingdon, Oxon, OX14 4RN

Routledge is an imprint of the Taylor & Francis Group, an informa business

ISBN: 978-1-032-79200-2 (hbk)
ISBN: 978-1-032-78655-1 (pbk)
ISBN: 978-1-003-49097-5 (ebk)

DOI: 10.4324/9781003490975

Typeset in Palatino
by SPi Technologies India Pvt Ltd (Straive)

Contents

Acknowledgements

I would like to express my sincere gratitude to every teacher and administrator I have worked with throughout my career. Every one of you has taught me so much. Your strengths have shone a light on my Blindspots, and for that I will always be grateful. Thank you to my wonderful editor, Lauren Davis: you knew exactly what to say and how to say it to make this book a reality, and to Stephen Poole, whose detailed work is so much appreciated. Thank you to my readers Ali Powell and Kate Bonnycastle, love you both! Special thanks to my mentors Lois Rowe, Tony Araujo, and John Fauntley: your example has always been my gold standard.

Meet the Author

Dr. Anne Bonnycastle has been working as a teacher, administrator, department head, and instructional coach in both public and independent schools since 1996. She has taught social studies, English Language Arts, economics, accounting, band, choir, orchestra, and general music. Anne has delivered professional development sessions on assessment practices, classroom management, and student voice. Throughout her long and varied career, she has been a professional development junkie, completing an MA in educational psychology and a Doctoral degree in Music Education.

Anne lives in Vancouver with her husband: both are adjusting well to being empty-nesters. When she isn't teaching, you can find Anne cold plunging in the ocean, enjoying too many cups of coffee, or playing piano in a local cocktail bar.

Part I

Blindspots

Introduction

> Positive change can best be accomplished if one constantly monitors and questions one's teaching practice. — Michael Huberman (1992)

McKinsey & Company, one of the world's pre-eminent global consulting firms, studied 25 school systems across the globe to find out why some school systems consistently perform well and improve faster than others (Barber & Mourshed, 2007). After a massive research program involving thousands of interviews, data analyses, and literature reviews, they discovered that teacher development was the key. The overall conclusion was that "the only way to improve outcomes is to improve instruction" (p. 7).

Improving instruction. That is what this book is about. Not improving other people's instruction – improving your own. Because at the end of the day, professional development, teacher assessment and evaluation, courses, books – none of it will do us any good unless we take the time to look our practice squarely in the face and ask "What can I do better? What am I missing? What am I not seeing here?" As Michael Huberman (above) says, constant monitoring and questioning are the way forward.

Teacher growth and development are hard. Because it is personal. It is not one-size-fits-all. And the toughest thing about it is that the one thing everybody needs in order to grow – honest, helpful, and clear feedback – is almost impossible to get.

If you are a teacher who wants to grow as a professional, you need access to clear, honest feedback about where you are now, so you can do what you need to do to get where you need to go. But feedback – the helpful kind of feedback that will support

DOI: 10.4324/9781003490975-2

your growth – is scarce. Your administrators are unlikely to give it to you – certainly not the hard, personal, and game-changing kind, because that can sound like criticism. Your colleagues aren't going to give it to you, because chances are, they value positive relationships more than your professional development. In schools, where we strive to create cultures of positivity and support, real feedback can be pretty hard to find.

If you work in a school where you have an annual scheduled teacher evaluation, that may be your one opportunity to access feedback from your administrator. In my experience, however, school administrators are so overloaded with other work that the annual observation frequently goes by the wayside, especially for more experienced teachers. In any case, owing to time constraints, the evaluation process may consist of your being observed for only one – or part of one – teaching block. Typically, your observer then fills out a teacher evaluation form and meets with you to discuss your growth needs. This process produces a list of things you are doing right, and then may very gently suggest one small tweak. That small tweak may or may not be helpful, depending on whether the class that was observed was at all representative of your teaching.

More likely, however, teacher evaluation conversations will focus on your own self-assessment. You may have been given a list of criteria on which to base your self-assessment. This approach is rooted in the belief that you know your teaching best – so you are in the best position to assess your work. This may or may not be true. The fact of the matter is that your instructional leader's primary objective for these meetings is to make you feel supported and acknowledged.

This is why the self-assessment model is so popular. If your administrator delegates the job of providing constructive criticism to you, they don't run the risk of making you feel disrespected. So sure, teachers' egos stay unbruised; however, honest, constructive feedback doesn't emerge. You will never know what you can't see: your teaching blindspots stay hidden from you. As a result, you can never address the one thing that would make a tremendous difference to your teaching.

What your administrators believe. Having been a school administrator, I can tell you that being tasked with improving the quality of instruction is a very difficult job. As an administrator, you need to find a way to help the teachers under your jurisdiction teach better – without interrupting what they are doing well, making them feel "less than," or overwhelming them with too many new ideas. Most importantly, you need to earn and keep your teachers' trust. You need to be supportive, affirming, and kind.

The easiest way out, for an administrator, is ***not*** to point out individuals' teaching weaknesses at all. This is a choice I have often made when I've been in the administrator's seat. Instead, in those one-on-one teacher evaluation meetings, I focus on what the teacher is doing well. As for growth opportunities – I hope the teacher has the self-awareness and motivation to identify those for themselves, rather than my running the risk of appearing critical and hurting our working relationship. In any case (the thinking goes), teachers will only work on things that ***they*** think are important, so there is no value in pointing things out to them that they don't self-identify.

This, despite all the research that shows we are not good at self-assessment!

The Dunning–Kruger effect – the less we know, the more we think we know (Kruger & Dunning, 1999) – is, according to research, alive and well in teacher practice (e.g., Krause, 2022; Ernst et al., 2023). This is why Blindspots prevail.

What about Whole-School Professional Development?

> Nothing has promised so much and has been so frustratingly wasteful as the thousands of workshops and conferences that led to no significant change in practice when the teachers returned to their classrooms. — Fullan (1991, p. 315)

Like Fullan (above), I have rarely found whole-school professional development to be an effective vehicle for teacher growth. While it can address topics such as curriculum, unit planning, or assessment – the *what* of teaching – it fails to address the really important aspects of teaching: ***how*** teachers are teaching in their classrooms on a day-by-day basis. Because the ***how*** of teaching is individual, it cannot be addressed by a one-size-fits-all solution.

I have been on both the providing and the receiving end of whole-staff professional development, and I have yet to see a program that has been able to meet the needs of an entire teaching staff. It just makes no sense to spend the time and energy of so many people on high-level topics that some are already experts at, while others would be better served by developing more fundamental skills. No matter how cleverly you deliver the Pro-D (make it interactive, put teachers into small groups, bring in guest speakers) – you're going to miss the mark with most of the teachers. You certainly won't be addressing the things most important to your teachers' development, **because everyone has different needs**.

This is the concern – that teachers are not getting the professional development they need – that led me to write *Find Your Blindspot in the Classroom*. The best teachers I know are self-aware ones. I wanted to discover how we can all develop that high level of self-awareness – even when we don't have access to an instructional coach or an individually tailored professional development program.

About Me

I have been teaching and working as an administrator, department head, and instructional coach in both public and independent schools since 1996. I have taught social studies, English Language Arts, economics, and music. I've directed choirs, orchestras, and bands and written and directed dozens of school musicals. I've taught mommy-and-me music classes and conducted a community band for retired seniors. I've lectured at the university level on accounting and taxation. I have delivered professional development on assessment practices, classroom management, and student voice. Throughout my long and varied career, I have been, consistently, a professional development junkie.

Wanting to be the very best teacher I could be, I have attended endless workshops and conferences and completed an MA in educational psychology to improve my teaching. When I stepped into a leadership position, I doubled down on my professional learning: read every book I could get my hands on, earned my doctoral degree, and took courses in coaching, team building, and change management. I spoke with teacher leaders and school administrators, listened to podcasts (#Tom Schimmer), asked thousands of questions, and spoke with anyone willing to listen to help me figure it out. (Figure what out? All of it.)

The biggest professional challenge I have ever encountered is helping other teachers develop in a lasting and meaningful way. Fostering growth and development in others is really hard – and, in some ways, impossible: substantive professional growth can only ever be self-driven. We can support and coach others and provide resources, time, recommendations and encouragement. But in the end, teacher professional growth must be initiated and driven by teachers themselves. This led me to the question: **What does it take to grow and develop?**

Decades of research and reflection into this question led me to the key: **self-awareness**. The one thing I know for sure is that the best teachers are the ones who are self-aware. The ones who constantly scan their teaching, question their thinking, and actively seek out Blindspots in their practice: these teachers are the ones who produce the best results in their classrooms.

I have seen it in action, over and over again: the teacher who critically observes what is happening in their classroom, wonders why things happen the way they do, tries out different approaches, thinks about it, jots things down in a notebook, actively seeks out feedback, and is always asking the question: "Is there a better way?" – these characteristics abound in the most effective teachers.

On the other hand, teachers who have all the answers, who are sure of themselves, and who rarely ask for feedback: these are the teachers whom I notice don't grow in their practice. These are the teachers whose students could be served better. And this, I believe, is where the untapped potential lies: rather than trying to impose Pro-D directly, **first raise teacher self-awareness**, then let teachers drive their own professional growth.

What This Book Will Do for You

In this book, I take a deficit-mastery approach. This may sound a bit harsh, but it is meant to help us uncover the issues that most need addressing in your own teaching practice – efficiently and effectively. I start by listing (and describing) the 10 Classic Blindspots: the things that I have frequently observed needing attention in teachers' practice and that I know, when addressed, deliver the best results for teachers and their students.

I have observed hundreds of teachers, and I have noticed that the same ten issues come up again and again. No matter the level of experience, the subject, or the age group taught, the pattern is clear: almost every teacher (including me) seems to be missing one of these pieces of the puzzle. I call these areas "Blindspots" because it is clear that we are not aware of the impact these issues have on our students and our teaching. We are not aware, because if we knew better, we would do better.

With Part I of this book, you have in your hand a list of these ten common Blindspots. These are research-supported aspects of teaching that – once you address them – will have a significant impact on your students' learning. Part I dives into each of the Blindspots in detail, providing anecdotes and supporting research.

Once you know what the Classic 10 Blindspots are, you can then identify which Blindspot is yours. But how do you see the unseeable? **How do you discover your Blindspot?**

Part II of this book provides six different ways that you can obtain data to help you find your Blindspot. Six different strategies that, in combination, will help you to detect clues, identify patterns, and see trends. Put together, this data will point to that one aspect of your teaching where you can dig into for professional development gold.

Is one of the strategies "ask your administrator?" No. Because chances are, your administrator won't tell you straight up what you need to fix. The research shows that principals rarely deliver negative feedback (e.g., Yariv, 2006; Dobbelaer, Prins, & van Dongen, 2013). Think about the last time you sat with an administrator to talk about your practice. My guess is you received advice, praise, and evaluation – but no real feedback. And, if you're like me, the last thing you want is to bring up the topic of your shortcomings with someone who has hiring and firing powers.

So, no, the strategies in this book are here to help you discover – **for yourself** – what your Blindspot is. You won't have to rely on an instructional coach (which you probably don't have) or your administrator (which you may not want to do). You will need help from a critical, trusted colleague for Strategy #3 (Forced Choice). And you will have to elicit your students' opinions for Strategy #4 (Student Input). However, Part II of this book walks you through all six strategies in a way that (hopefully) feels comfortable and painless. By simply putting two or three of the strategies in this book together, you can raise your self-awareness and get a sense of where your one Blindspot is.

Only one. Notice that I refer to Blindspot in the singular. Although we all may have multiple Blindspots, that's not the point. The point is to find **the one** that is most critical to our development as teachers. As human beings, we can address only one thing at a time. (Chase too many rabbits, and they all get away, as the saying goes.) The goal here is to figure out what the priority is: Which single Blindspot, when addressed, will have the biggest, most significant impact on our students' learning? The other areas can wait until we've dealt with this one.

And then what? When you have figured out which Blindspot is the most critical for you, it is no longer a Blindspot. So now we call it something else: your Professional Practice Focus (PPF).

Even though just figuring out where you need to focus your attention is a tremendous accomplishment – and the reason I wrote this book – I have given you some next steps in Part III.

For each PPF, Part III suggests how you can begin to address this facet of your practice. There are mountains of resources, entire books, courses, and scads of research literature full of advice, strategies, and tools for each PPF; however, Part III shows you how to begin, plus provides recommendations for where to go for more resources. As long as you have accurately identified your Blindspot, you will be able to up your game significantly with only the suggestions in this book, along with your own determination and commitment to growth.

And then, after a month, or a term, or a year of working on this aspect of your teaching, you may feel ready to look for your next Blindspot. In that case, you can reread this book, and start the process over again!

References

Barber, M., & Mourshed, M. (2007). *How the world's best-performing school systems come out on top*. McKinsey & Company.

Dobbelaer, M. J., Prins, F. J., & van Dongen, D. (2013). The impact of feedback training for inspectors. *European Journal of Training and Development*, *37*(1), 86–104.

Ernst, H. M., Wittwer, J., & Voss, T. (2023). Do they know what they know? Accuracy in teacher candidates' self-assessments and its influencing factors. *British Educational Research Journal*, *49*(4), 649–673.

Fullan M.G. (1991). *The new meaning of educational change* (2nd ed). Teachers College Press.

Huberman, M. (1992). Teacher development and instructional mastery. In A. Hargreaves & M. Fullan (Eds.), *Understanding teacher development* (pp. 122–142). Teachers' College Press.

Krause, R. (2022, June). Teacher competence in relation to the overconfidence effect. In *IAI Academic Conference Proceedings* (p. 45). International Academic Institute.

Kruger, J., & Dunning, D. (1999). Unskilled and unaware of it: How difficulties in recognizing one's own incompetence lead to inflated self-assessments. *Journal of Personality and Social Psychology*, *77*(6), 1121.

Yariv, E. (2006). Mum effect: Principals' reluctance to submit negative feedback. *Journal of Managerial Psychology*, *21*(6), 533–546. https://doi.org/10.1108/02683940610684382

1

Why You Need This Book

> What matters is *how* things are taught, rather than *what* is taught.
> — Dylan Wiliam (2011)

Ashley had been teaching for three years. She was enthusiastic, keen, and smart. She loved her subject – history – and she loved the idea of creating a warm, inviting classroom environment for her grade 10 Social Studies students. She wanted to present as the kind, friendly teacher she never had when she was a kid. Ashley smiled a lot, laughed at her students' jokes, and went to great pains to make her lesson plans fun, easy, and kid-friendly. She wanted everyone to feel successful in her class.

The problem was that her students weren't buying it.

They were high-schoolers and felt like they were being treated like third graders. They found Ashley's voice overly sweet and her constant cheeriness forced. When she couldn't be heard over the classroom noise, Ashley raised the pitch of her voice as well as the volume, adopting a sing-song cadence and child-like language. She tended to repeat the same instructions over and over again. Her students had learned to tune her out.

Ashley wanted to be accommodating, so she gave extension after extension for assignments and was easily persuaded to delay tests. Her students had learned to simply ignore her

DOI: 10.4324/9781003490975-3

constant pleading to do their homework, stop talking, and pay attention. Ashley found that a unit she had planned for five weeks took nine weeks to complete. By the end of the year, she was frustrated by how little material they had covered.

When I had a chance to sit in on her class, I could feel Ashley's frustration. Despite her efforts to be nice, helpful, and friendly, her students were not engaged. More than one student spent the period playing video games on their open laptop. Three students signed out to go to the bathroom and never returned (they had gone out to shoot hoops on the basketball court). Constant chatter and noise removed any sense of order and progress. The work they were supposed to be doing was well below the grade 10 level. Ashley's attempts to engage the students with questions drew either no response or joke answers. It was clear that Ashley's students weren't learning in her class.

As Head of Academics, I was responsible for helping Ashley – and all the other teachers on staff – raise their game. So I did what I was trained to do: engage Ashley in a coaching conversation, in which she would identify what was going well in her teaching, what was tricky for her, and what she would like to work on going forward. My assignment was to support her in developing those aspects of her teaching that she had identified for herself.

What was going well? Ashley thought her students were beginning to share her passion for history.

What was tricky? She was trying to incorporate Universal Design for Learning (UDL) into her lesson planning (this was a new initiative the principal had introduced) and was still getting used to the new unit planning template.

What would she like to work on going forward? She wanted to incorporate more content related to Indigenous peoples' experiences and voices. Ashley was thinking about attending an upcoming professional development workshop called "Bringing Indigenous Knowledge into the Classroom."

Yes. Absolutely. Engage in the school's UDL curriculum initiative. And yes. We need all of our teachers to bring Indigenous knowledge, perspectives, and voices into the classroom. One hundred percent.

However. What about the issues right in front of her? The fact is, like Dylan Wiliam said (above), it doesn't matter ***what*** you teach if ***how*** you teach isn't working. And in Ashley's class, the *how* wasn't cutting it. Students were not learning. No amount of UDL or Indigenous content was going to make a difference.

Ideally, Ashley and I would have had a meaningful discussion about the biggest issues limiting Ashley's best efforts. Ashley didn't realize that the way she was speaking to the class had a tremendous impact. A few direct, simple strategies (e.g., modulating volume, lowering pitch, using wait time effectively, and employing an effective classroom management plan) could turn Ashley's class around.

Unfortunately, the professional development model I was working under restricted me from pointing out flaws, highlighting weaknesses, or exposing things about a teacher's practice that they themselves did not raise. I could support, affirm, and provide resources for the things ***Ashley*** wanted to address. But if Ashley didn't bring something up herself, I did not have the prerogative to point it out.

Ashley clung tightly to the belief she was a fabulous teacher but wrestled with the constant challenge of the lack of order, achievement, and progress in her classroom. She doubled down on her habits, thinking more of the same would somehow provide better results. She developed a reputation among students – unbeknownst to her – as an easy marker, a cloying instructor, and a pushover.

It would have taken multiple hours, over many weeks, to gently help Ashley break through her lack of self-awareness and identify her counterproductive habits without fracturing her ego. A skilled instructional coach could have done it, by having regular one-on-one coaching conversations with Ashley over a long period of time. By asking a series of carefully nuanced questions, the coach could have guided Ashley in the direction she needed to go. Ultimately, after many sessions, Ashley may have realized that she had some changes she needed to make.

However, this was not the work nor the timeline I was asked to take on. Nor was it the long-term journey of improvement that Ashley requested. Teaching is unbelievably busy work. Instruction, marking, preparing, communications with parents, staff meetings, department meetings, report cards, extra-curriculars … there is barely time to go to the bathroom, let alone time to sit with an instructional coach for a couple of hours a week for months, and slowly, gently, peel away the layers toward self-awareness.

Schools don't have the budget for this subtle, nuanced work. Few have access to a dedicated instructional coach who is skilled in gently probing, questioning, and leading – over weeks, months, even years – individual teachers along the path to self-awareness. Instead, the job of supporting teacher growth typically falls to an administrator. Administrators can be superheroes, but few are trained in the subtle art of therapeutic coaching. Regardless, they don't have the time, with everything else on their plate.

School administrators are lucky if they have the time to give their staff one teaching observation a year. Many of the schools I have worked at were able to provide individual teachers with a one-off teaching observation once every three years. Typically, these observations are tied to teacher evaluation, so that any resulting feedback is coupled with assessment. Combining honest feedback with evaluation makes the whole experience highly fraught with emotion and anxiety. It just doesn't work. Furthermore, principals hate this process as much as teachers do and, to avoid damaging the relationship, will typically not mention teaching flaws, according to research (Yariv, 2006).

No wonder self-assessment forms the basis of teacher evaluation: Only you have the breadth of time in your classroom to truly know what is going on. Only you can know the intricacies of what you are trying to achieve, moment to moment in your class. And self-evaluation protects your administrator from the risks of seeming over-critical.

Except that self-evaluation leaves Blindspots. If you can't see it, you can't fix it. Ashley certainly couldn't see hers. She was not aware that her sing-songy voice grated on her students and that they had learned to tune her out. How do we know she wasn't aware of this? **Because if she were aware, she would have fixed it**. Like us all, Ashley wanted to be the best teacher she could be. If she knew better, she would have done better.

Martine was another teacher I worked with. Knowledgeable and experienced, Martine exuded warmth and kindness and yet she maintained firm control. Students sat quietly in her class. They worked diligently. They listened to her when she talked – and she talked a lot. She delivered instruction through PowerPoint slides accompanied by lengthy commentary. Frequently, she elaborated with interesting, but rambling, anecdotes. Throughout, her students sat quietly, appearing to listen even when their attention wandered – because it must have. I know mine did when I sat in Martine's class.

When Martine asked a question of the class, very few hands went up. Martine believed that her students were very shy, had few ideas, and perhaps lacked confidence in their opinions because they clearly didn't like talking in her class. (She should have observed them in Ashley's class!) The occasional times that a student did respond with a brief one-word answer, Martine would rephrase (at length) what the student had said and then provide the correct answer.

Martine's students would get more out of her class, and she out of her students, if she could learn to talk less and engage students in dialogue. Simple to do, but not easy. I knew of countless tools, techniques, and strategies that would have helped Martine adjust her style and, over time, engage her students more actively in their learning. She just needed to know that this was a priority she could address.

But I was not in a position to tell Martine this directly, just as I was not able to help Ashley.

However, there was a significant difference in what happened next. After I sat in Martine's class, she pulled me aside and said: "I want to know how to improve my teaching. What can I do to be better?"

I was unused to such an outright request for feedback, and I wasn't sure how to handle it. So, I started my usual feedback sandwich, beginning with things that were going well – but she cut me off. "No, I don't want to hear about that stuff," she said. "Get to the point. Tell me how I can do better."

In all my years of leadership in schools, I had never had a teacher ask me, point blank, for critical feedback. I was flummoxed. Despite her request, I was still hesitant. People may say they want to hear the criticism, but do they really?

As it happened, I had presented my Blindspots idea, still in its infancy, at an earlier staff meeting. That is, I had shared with my staff the eight areas that we would focus on throughout the year in Pro-D sessions – these were eight general issues I had seen across the school that were problematic in teachers' practice. I was not planning to call out any teacher with specifics. This was merely to support teachers' self-assessment. They could then choose ***for themselves***, from the eight, the area they wished to work on, and I would provide professional development support for each area.

Martine pulled out that list. Then she asked me the magic question: "Which one of these is mine?" She was not asking me if she was a good teacher. She was not asking for an evaluation of any kind. She was simply asking me to point out one thing – the one thing that, if she were to address it, would have a significant impact on her teaching and on her students' learning: the one thing that she was not seeing, the thing she was not aware of. Because we both knew, if she were aware of it, she would have fixed it.

In that moment, I realized that **Martine had shown me a way to help teachers find their Blindspot while keeping their ego intact**. I pointed to item #3 on the list and said gently, "I think this would make a big difference." (#3 was "Reduce teacher talk, increase student talk".) She thanked me. She asked for resources. She asked which teachers in the school could she observe who did this well. She asked me to come in and coach her on this one thing. Within a month or two, Martine, already a wonderful, well-loved, and knowledgeable teacher, had taken her practice to the next level.

Martine taught me that what teachers need is a simple list of the things that typically evade teachers' self-awareness. A concise collection of the most commonly occurring Blindspots in teacher practice. I dove into the research. I had observed hundreds of teachers and had a sense of the most commonly occurring Blindspot candidates; now I wanted to broaden my research and hone my ideas.

I started with John Hattie's *Visible Learning* (2008) and *Visible Learning: The Sequel* (2023), a synthesis of more than 800 meta-studies about what works best in schools. Hattie's work covers more than 80 million students worldwide. Then I dug into the studies cited within Hattie's research and, from there, explored research literature related to best teaching practices, teacher development, and teacher evaluation. After a two-year search, I refined the list of the Classic Ten Blindspots that seem to lie outside teachers' awareness but that will have the most impact once addressed. Part I of this book lists and discusses each of these in detail, citing the relevant research.

Knowing what the commonly occurring Blindspots are is the first step. Figuring out which one applies to you – when by definition, a Blindspot lies outside your awareness – that's another story. If, like most, you teach in a school that does not provide regular, frequent observation and feedback by a trained instructional coach, you need some way to identify your Blindspot for yourself. Part II of this book gives you strategies to do just that: Flip the Coin, Sit in Others' Classrooms, Forced Choice, Using Student Input, The Camera Doesn't Lie, and Self-Reflection. Using some or all of these strategies in combination will triangulate your evidence and lead you to discover your Blindspot – without destroying your confidence, while keeping your ego intact.

Once you know which Blindspot is yours, you can address it. Part III of this book shows you how to get started. Again, backed by research, I have curated what I have found to be the best resources, tools, and strategies to develop each of these particular areas of teacher practice.

Self-awareness requires looking at ourselves squarely, honestly – warts and all. It is hard work, painful at times – but worth it. This book will give you the tools to do this work in a way that leaves you feeling whole, so that you can give your students your very best.

We are all flawed – awesomely so. We all have things we are really great at. And we all have Blindspots. The goal of this book is to help you identify those things that you can't see that will have a significant impact on your teaching effectiveness, for the sake of your students. Because that is the reason we do anything – to give our students the best we possibly can.

The goal here is not to become a perfect teacher – the goal is to become **better**. I want you to celebrate, expand, and enjoy those aspects of teaching that you know you do well and to attend to the things that are getting in your way. Better teaching, better learning, better you. One Blindspot at a time.

References

Hattie, J. (2008). *Visible learning*. Routledge.

Hattie, J. (2023). *Visible learning: the sequel*. Routledge.

Wiliam, D. (2011). *Embedded formative assessment*. SolutionTree Press.

Yariv, E. (2006). Mum effect: Principals' reluctance to submit negative feedback. *Journal of Managerial Psychology*, *21*(6), 533–546.

2

The Classic Ten Blindspots

The basics are how it's done. — Dana K. White (2019)

The Ten Blindspots I have listed and described in this chapter are basic. They are not complicated, new, or earth-shattering. You have encountered them all before, in teacher-education programs, in textbooks, and in training sessions. But as Dana White says, the basics are how anything gets done. From my observations of hundreds of amazing and fabulous teachers, and from conversations with principals, instructional coaches, and school leaders, I have found that these very basic aspects of teaching are precisely the ones that we cannot see for ourselves.

These Blindspots are the *hows* of teaching, and because they are so personal, no one is pointing them out to us. These are the lettuce in the teeth, the open fly, the toilet paper on the shoe of teaching. And these are the things that need to be attended to first, before we tackle the *what* of teaching: weighty matters like curriculum, assessment, and pedagogical Big Ideas.

Do you ever wish you had a friend, colleague, or coach who would tell you, to your face, the one thing you need to change, the one thing that would have the most impact on your teaching practice? I never had that person, in all my years of teaching, and I certainly never had the audacity to deliver this kind of news

DOI: 10.4324/9781003490975-4

to any of my colleagues. As an administrator and instructional coach, I have worked with teacher feedback and evaluation systems that would never permit me to come right out and say, "You have a Blindspot, and this is it." And, in all my years, I only ever had one teacher ask me directly to identify their Blindspot.

Just One Blindspot

Let me assure you: You do not have all of these Blindspots. The Blindspots don't co-vary: having one tends to mean you don't have certain other ones. Typically, in any teacher's practice, there is really only one Blindspot that needs priority attention.

Yes, there may be a few items from the list that would be worth addressing in your practice. But you don't need to change everything at once. Addressing your number one Blindspot will have an immediate and significant impact on the quality of your teaching. Start with the low-hanging fruit! Your challenge right now is to identify your priority. Part II of this book provides strategies to help you uncover which one most applies to your teaching. Once you know which Blindspot applies to you – good news! It is no longer a Blindspot, and you can move forward knowing where to spend your professional development time and energy.

A Word about the Research

My curated list of Blindspots is supported by research, summarized as I discuss each one, below. You will see me referring frequently to John Hattie's work *Visible Learning* (Hattie, 2003, Hattie & Yates, 2013, Hattie, 2023) and his 2003 paper "Teachers make a difference: What is the research evidence?"

John Hattie's Visible Learning Research. John Hattie's research is based on such a vast quantity of data that I relied on it heavily to support my initial list of Blindspots. Hattie's research program was driven by the question: Which variables have the greatest impact on student achievement? To answer this question, Hattie (2023) examined over 2103 meta-analyses of more than 130,000 empirical research studies on the attributes of successful teaching and learning in schools. The result of this large-data inquiry is a list of 357 factors, ranked by level of influence, that affect student achievement. Check out the results at Visible Learning Meta^{x} (https://www.visiblelearningmetax.com), the largest global online database of What Works Best in Education.

Hattie grouped the 357 factors into major areas of influence: student, home, school, teacher, classroom, and curricula. For example, the factors that relate to students' home environment (e.g., single-parent family, parents out of work) are grouped under the domain "home." What students bring to the table (e.g., a growth mindset, work habits) are grouped under the domain "students." It turns out that factors under the teacher's control have the strongest combined effect. As Hattie himself put it, "excellence in teaching is the single most powerful influence on achievement" (Hattie, 2003, p. 4).

Effect size. Hattie's method produced an effect size for each of the Visible Learning factors, showing the relative strength of each factor on student learning. A positive effect size means that the factor is associated with positive student outcomes (good!). A negative effect size means that the factor is associated with negative student outcomes (bad!). The average effect size is a positive 0.4, which Hattie considers to be the "hinge point." Any positive effect size above 0.4, he explains, is likely to accelerate student learning above and beyond the status quo. Therefore, factors with effect sizes between 0 and 0.4 are probably not that significant.

An example is "playing background music in the class." Sometimes, I'll play classical music when students are trying to focus. I'm sure I've read somewhere that this helps students' spatial reasoning or something like that. But it turns out, after combining data from 79 studies involving 3,104 students, Hattie calculated that Background Music has an effect size of 0.1. So, in fact, it doesn't have a *significant* positive effect. I won't argue with my students that it does, and I will continue to do it when it feels right.

The Blindspots in my curated list align with factors from the Visible Learning research – factors (unlike Background Music) that do make a difference. And I didn't take Hattie at his word – I dug into the studies that underlie the meta-analyses on which Hattie's effect sizes are based, so that I could really understand what is going on.

Hattie's (2003) paper "Teachers Make a Difference, What is the research evidence?" identified the differences between expert teachers and experienced teachers. In other words, Hattie didn't just compare the practices of new teachers to experienced teachers, he looked at really excellent teachers and compared them to teachers who simply had years under their belts. I found that this work, though 20 years old, was tremendously helpful in fine-tuning the Classic Ten Blindspots, as you will see as we go through the list.

Beyond Hattie's Visible Learning research program, there is a wealth of research that I drew on to refine the Blindspot list. Without further ado, then, here they are:

10 Blindspots: What No One Is Telling You about Your Teaching Practice

1. Cut the words – Reduce teacher talk, increase student talk.
2. Fix verbal hazards – Check shrillness, meekness, repetitive phrases, sounding too young, and upspeak.
3. Loosen the reins – Stop micromanaging – students are more capable than you think.
4. Dial back overpreparation – Be more responsive to student needs.
5. Get organized – Provide students with clarity, consistency, and accountability.
6. Use every minute – Stop wasting time.
7. Set boundaries – Students need a teacher, not a BFF.
8. Move the bar – Set an appropriate level of challenge.
9. Make it safe to make mistakes – Create a positive "error culture."
10. Like them all – Show students you're on their side.

What Is the Relationship between Blindspots?

This list was designed for you to identify a **single** behavior that could be your Blindspot: the one thing that, if addressed, would have **the most impact** on your students' learning and experience. Of the hundreds of teachers I've worked with, all would benefit tremendously from addressing one of these Blindspots. If only we knew which one applied!

These Classic Ten Blindspots are meant to operate independently. Each one could exist solely in a teacher's practice, without any of the others. In fact, some of these Blindspots tend to exclude others. A teacher with Blindspot #4 (Check Overpreparation) would not likely also have Blindspot #7 (Use Every Minute) or Blindspot #6 (Get Organized). A teacher with Blindspot #2 (Loosen the Reins) is unlikely to also have #5 (Set Boundaries). But you never know.

On the other hand, some Blindspots could well appear together. Certainly, I have noticed that teachers who would benefit from talking less (#1 – Cut the Words) tend to be inefficient with class time (#7 – Use Every Minute). Teachers who need to Loosen the Reins (#2) often need to also Check Overpreparation (#4); however, I still advise against trying to identify more than one Blindspot at a time for your practice.

Identify just one (using the tools in section 2) and focus on that one. Make it a priority. Chapter 6 (Forced Choice) capitalizes on this concept of prioritization to help teachers focus on the one, and only one, Blindspot that, when addressed, will have the most significant impact on their students' learning experience. The goal here is not to be the perfect teacher. **The goal is to be a better teacher tomorrow than you are today**. One Blindspot at a time.

1 Cut the Words: Reduce Teacher Talk, Increase Student Talk

In my experience as a teacher, as an observer of teaching, and as a researcher, the most prevalent teacher behavior that detracts from student learning is Too Much Teacher Talk. This one can be very difficult to see in ourselves. Rare is the teacher who knows that they talk too much.

The fact of the matter is teachers love to talk. We enjoy giving lengthy explanations, delivering detailed instructions, sharing our expansive subject knowledge – it gives us the feeling that we're doing our job. Teaching *is* talking, isn't it?

Well, no. Every second that the teacher is talking is a second that students are not involved in active learning activities. Research shows that when teachers talk too much, students check out (Gharbavi & Iravani, 2014). When teachers talk too much, students' voices are diminished. They lose agency. They lose time to think and reflect. They lose opportunities to develop their own thinking through writing, problem-solving, classroom conversations, discussions, and discourse (Hattie, 2012; Kostadinovska-Stojchevska & Popovikj, 2019).

Blindspot #1 occurs when teachers talk too much.

So, how much is too much?

The fact is, teaching is a complex art. Waring (2021) calls it a "multifaceted juggling act" (p. 284) and explained that Teacher Talk is required for instructional, organizational, and socializing purposes. Teachers need to establish and manage interactions within the class, organize and supervise classroom activities, transmit knowledge, provide assistance – all of which require talking. The ideal amount of Teacher Talk depends entirely on the context. Having said that, researchers Kostadinovska-Stojchevska and Popovikj (2019) recommend that teachers limit their talking time to 20% to 30% of class time. More than this, they suggest, can lead to negative effects.

John Hattie's Visible Learning research found that "Classroom Discussion" – which you could say is the opposite of Teacher Talk – had an effect size of 0.82, meaning it has a "potential to considerably accelerate" student learning. Hattie explained that classroom discussion involves students discussing with each other, prompted from an open (not closed) set of questions. At the same time, "Lectures" (the epitome of Teacher Talk) had an effect size of –0.26, meaning "likely to have a negative impact" (Hattie, 2023). Clearly, a shift away from "talking at" students, and a shift toward engaging students in discourse and other active learning activities, has proven benefits.

The Teacher Talk issue seems to be one that eludes teacher self-awareness. Studies have shown that the amount of teacher talk predicted by teachers prior to analysis differed alarmingly from actual measurement (e.g., Kostadinovska-Stojchevska & Popovikj, 2019). Many teachers truly lack awareness of how much their voice dominates the classroom – I've been in classrooms where students simply stop listening, check out, and become passive – while teachers are unable to pinpoint the cause of the issue. In these cases, teachers' practice would benefit tremendously by

a) Being more concise in the talking they do
b) Designing learning activities to include more pair and group work
c) Developing productive classroom discussion that is student-centered and less teacher-centered
d) Honing teaching skills of wait-time and questioning techniques
e) Exploring alternatives to transmitting knowledge via lecture or teacher demonstration.

All of these adjustments can reduce the number of minutes that students are required to listen to Teacher Talk – without compromising student learning.

I feel compelled to mention vocal health here. Research shows that teachers, more than the general population, are at risk for health problems related to vocal overuse (Morton & Watson, 1998). Martins et al. (2014) estimated the prevalence of voice disorders among the general population is 6%–15%, compared to teachers at 20%–50%, reaching up to 80% in some schools. These health problems can include chronic upper respiratory diseases, hypertonic neck muscles, and gastroesophageal reflux, as well as voice deterioration, and, ultimately, lesions on the vocal cords (De Alvear et al., 2011). Teachers with voice disorders are more likely to exhibit absenteeism (Van Houtte et al., 2011) and burnout syndrome (De Brito Mota et al., 2019). It behooves us to incorporate healthy vocal techniques into our teaching – starting with strategically talking less.

To demonstrate the magic of economy when it comes to Teacher Talk, consider John Wooden, widely regarded as the greatest teacher of basketball of all time. (Wooden was the creator of the "Pyramid of Success" – the inspiration for Ted Lasso's legendary coaching style.) A study of Wooden's methods by Gallimore and Tharp (2004) revealed the great coach's brevity: "Wooden's teaching utterances and comments were short, punctuated, and numerous. There were no lectures, no extended harangues … he rarely spoke longer than 20 seconds" (p. 120).

Chances are, if the amount of Teacher Talk is something you do think about regularly, self-reflect on, and intentionally consider as you plan and teach your classes, then this is not a Blindspot for you. On the other hand, if Teacher Talk is not something you actively address, then see Part II of this book, to help you to identify whether this Blindspot should be your priority.

2 Fix Verbal Hazards: Check Habits Like Shrillness, Lack of Presence, Repetitive Phrases, and Upspeak

Teachers – even those who actively minimize the amount that they do talk – must be able to communicate effectively to groups of students verbally. Verbal habits that impede communication ultimately undermine teachers' credibility. I call ineffective verbal habits "Verbal Hazards."

Who has ever had an administrator willing to deliver the feedback that their "baby voice" is not as cute as they think? Who has ever had a colleague brave enough to tell them that turning statements into questions (upspeak) provides poor role modeling for students? I have yet to meet a school administrator or instructional coach who has the courage to deliver such painfully honest news. This kind of tough love is personal and can cut deep. But addressing verbal hazards can have a profound impact on students. Unfortunately, Verbal Hazards (Blindspot #3) are typically left to the teacher to discover on their own. They rarely do.

Blindspot #2 occurs when verbal hazards erode credibility.
Hattie's Visible Learning research shows that "teacher credibility" has a whopping effect size of 1.09, meaning it has the potential to considerably accelerate learning (Visible Learning Meta^{x} website). Since Verbal Hazards definitely undermine teacher credibility, the impact of correcting this Blindspot can be very significant.

Verbal Hazards that I have observed include the following:

- Upspeak (or uptalk). Turning a declarative sentence or phrase into what sounds like a question is called upspeak. Users of upspeak are typically unaware they are doing it (Warren, 2016). Experts agree that upspeak is driven by a (conscious or unconscious) desire to come across as less harsh and more inviting. However, even when its use is subtle, upspeak signals a lack of confidence and a need for consensus (Tyler, 2015), and can undermine a teacher's credibility.
- Use of repetitive words or phrases. Overuse of a particular expression signals a lack of confidence. A common teacher foible is the overuse of a rhetorical "Ok?" at the end of phrases when giving instructions. Rather than making the instruction more inviting, which is presumably the intent, adding an "Ok?" at the end of every phrase actually signals uncertainty. Students know there is no option to respond "No, not ok." The result is that students sense insincerity, eroding trust and credibility. Other overused phrases I have heard include the repetitive use of "amazing!" By the fifth use of "amazing!" students roll their eyes and start to check out. Repetitive word use is beautifully illustrated by the famous scene in *Ferris Bueller's Day Off*: "Anyone? Anyone?"
- Overuse of the first-person plural when it isn't appropriate. The directive "Now we are going to write our name at the top of the worksheet!" comes across as insulting when the teacher is clearly not also filling out a worksheet. While the intention may be to make students feel invited to join in rather than directed ("We're all in this

together!"), the lack of authenticity feels patronizing. Students know that their job is to follow instructions and the teacher's job is to give them. Dressing instructions up as something else, again, undermines a teacher's credibility.

- Speaking with a shrill or too-loud tone of voice. Teachers may resort to this when attempting to be heard over classroom noise. Unfortunately, a tone that cuts through classroom noise ends up sounding harsh. Research shows that this tone of voice may be perceived by students as threatening, angry, or grating (Martin & Darnley, 2017). A better approach is to control classroom noise, wait for students' attention, and then speak in a tone that conveys warmth and confidence.
- Speaking in a monotone, lacking presence, or otherwise employing a sleep-inducing delivery. Again, the *Ferris Bueller* scene comes to mind. Perlman and McCann (1998) confirmed this in their research into aspects of teaching that students find annoying: number one on their list was a monotone, boring vocal delivery.
- Baby voice. This is an affected use of the high-pitched voice of prepubescent girls. It functions to set up a child-like persona, making the user sound cute and young (Jang, 2021). Presumably, teachers speak this way to make them seem more relatable to students. Unfortunately, teachers using childlike vocal inflections run the risk of making students feel infantilized or talked down-to.
- Similarly, kidspeak. This is the sprinkling of speech with the language of young children. McWhorter (2019) described Kidspeak in depth and included examples such as "because" (as in "because … science!") and "All the things!" (as in "Don't worry, we'll make sure we do all the things!"). For the same reason that they use baby voice, teachers may use kidspeak to make themselves more relatable. They may feel it makes them less threatening because it signals that they are "one of the kids." However, overuse of kidspeak can sometimes undermine a teacher's credibility. See Blindspot #5: students need a teacher, not a buddy.

- Speaking too quickly, with too little space between phrases. Students need time to process information. Research shows that this is one of the most annoying teacher habits identified by university students (Miley & Gonsalves, 2003; Perlman & McCann, 1998).

A final – and delicate – version of Blindspot #2 relates to speaking the language of instruction fluently. If your first language is not the language of instruction, your students' inability to understand you may be impeding their learning. If you teach a language-reliant course, such as Social Studies or English Language Arts, or if you teach young children where language development is critical, then it is even more crucial that you be able to speak, read, and write fluently in the language of instruction. This is sensitive feedback that teaching coaches will avoid for fear of being politically incorrect or of otherwise causing harm. But if you are teaching in your second language, this would be a Blindspot to consider.

Teachers whose verbal habits hamper their credibility, communication, or relationships in the classroom are rarely aware that this is an issue. If they were, presumably they would already be taking action to correct it. Part II of this book offers ways to help you discover whether this is a Blindspot for you. Part III provides strategies to address the issue.

3 Loosen the Reins: Stop Micromanaging – Students Are More Capable than You Think

When I was a student teacher, good classroom management seemed to be the holy grail of successful teaching. Classrooms where control is tight tend to be classrooms with excellent systems, high expectations for student behavior, and superb organization. These are all important in a healthy, thriving classroom. However…

When control is too tight, there is a cost. Too-tight control can compromise student agency and student autonomy. It can weaken students' belief in their own abilities to make decisions, get things done, cope, and succeed.

Research shows that over-controlling teacher behavior leads to student demotivation, anxiety, and anger (Assor et al., 2005). Dr. Assor and his team at Ben Gurion University call directly controlling teacher behaviors, such as giving frequent directives, "Autonomy Suppressive Behaviors" (ASBs). They found that ASBs in teachers were linked to negative emotions and poor outcomes in fourth and fifth graders (Assor & Kaplan, 2001; Assor, Kaplan, & Roth, 2002).

The opposite of too-tight control is "Autonomy-Supportive Teaching" (Reeve and Cheon, 2021). What does Autonomy-Supportive Teaching look like? Letting the monkeys run the zoo? Not at all. Supporting student autonomy looks different at different grade levels, but it might include things like eliciting and acknowledging perspectives, supporting self-initiative, offering choice, allowing students to figure things out by themselves, and minimizing pressure and control. Autonomy-supportive teachers are curious, open, and flexible toward students. They take an interest in students' interests and preferences and are curious about what students are thinking and wanting. They are open to students' input and engagement signals, are flexible, and are willing to bend the lesson to align more with students' preferences (Vansteenkiste et al., 2019). We are talking about balance.

Blindspot #3 occurs when classroom control gets out of balance.

Of course, the optimal degree of control must fit the needs of the students. Younger students may need a tighter grip than older students. Larger classes may require firmer classroom management practices than smaller groups. Some students simply need closer guidance than others. Think of it as a spectrum: not enough teacher control leads to chaos, confusion, poor behaviors, lack of clarity, and wasted time. More control than is necessary quickly turns into micromanaging. In micromanaged environments, students feel that they are not trusted to make decisions – even small ones – for themselves. They become passive and dependent.

Teachers with Blindspot #3 tend to be those who believe in systems, organization, and classroom discipline. John Hattie, in his research of characteristics that distinguished expert teachers from experienced teachers, found that too often, experienced (i.e., not expert) teachers "attempt to dominate the situation, rather than being receptive to what the students need" (2003, p. 8). He observed that experienced (but not expert) teachers often act out of their own need to maintain control rather than making students' needs for growth, agency, and independence the priority.

The teacher with Blindspot #3 may be acting out anxiety. Psychologists use the term "over-functioning" to describe those who manage their anxiety by micromanaging (e.g., Smith, 2019). While over-functioning may effectively manage the teacher's anxiety, it has a detrimental impact on students. If loosening the reins feels like a terrifying thing to do, it might be worth considering whether this is a Blindspot for you.

4 Dial Back Overpreparation: Be More Responsive to Student Needs

Warning: This Blindspot is potentially heretical. We are trained in teacher education programs to be prepared. A popular teacher's blog advises:

> Preparation and planning are a critical component of effective teaching. Lack thereof will lead to failure. If anything, every teacher should be over-prepared. Good teachers are almost in a continuous state of preparation and planning. They are always thinking about the next lesson. The impact of preparation and planning is tremendous on student learning.
>
> (Meador, 2019)

I had a faculty advisor during my teacher education practicum who required me to make lesson plans so detailed they were effectively a word-for-word script of what I was going to say. He required a time line, by the minute, of how the lesson would progress. This level of detail helped me to "cut the words" (see Blindspot #1) as I had to consider every word ahead of time. In the classroom, however, I felt unable to respond effectively to the students in front of me, because I had invested so much into the plan, and felt compelled to stick to it.

As in-service teachers, we are typically evaluated on our level of preparation. For example, the Marzano and Toth (2013) *Teacher Evaluation Model* has – of four domains – an entire domain called "Planning and Preparation," which includes items like "Planning and preparing for effective scaffolding of information within lessons" (p. 22). Similarly, Edwards' (2024) *Professional Development Courses for Teachers - Teacher Webinar* consists of four domains, one of which is also titled "Planning and Preparation." Full-time teachers are expected to work at least 8 hours a day: hours outside the (typically) 6 hours of teaching are meant for preparation and planning (along with all those other teacher tasks like marking and extracurriculars). Preparation is an important part of the job.

So, who in their right mind would ever suggest that there is such a thing as too much preparation?

Well, me. Because I have noticed that teachers who invest inordinate amounts of time in creating detailed plans are often the ones who do not respond as well to what really matters in classrooms: the students in front of them.

Blindspot #4 occurs when planning constrains responsiveness.

I have observed teachers who spend their weekends crafting beautiful PowerPoints, creating exquisite worksheets, scripting what they are intending to say and how and when they will say it, writing out detailed short- and long-term unit and lesson plans, building a complex scaffold of exactly what is going to happen. The result is that the teachers (a) burn out from all this work and (b) lack flexibility and responsiveness to the students in front of them, because they have invested so much into their plan. "I don't have time to answer that question (explore that idea, engage in that class discussion), because the plan requires us to get through these ten lessons before the unit test!"

In one case, a talented, intelligent teacher I was working with was clearly exhausted from spending late evenings and weekends creating detailed PowerPoint slides and strict minute-by-minute plans to accompany her lessons. Not only did I notice her stress from a lack work–life balance, but also I could see that she was not "reading the room" as well as she could. As I observed her students, it was clear to me that there were times her students needed more information; other times, less.

I asked her what would happen if she prepared less? What if she allowed the students the opportunity to ask questions? What if she were to follow their lead a little more? Gave them a little more choice, and herself a little more wiggle room?

From her response, I understood immediately that extensive preparation quelled the pervasive anxiety she still felt leading her classroom. Planning every minute of the lesson ahead of time kept her panic at bay. Unfortunately, it came at the cost of student voice and agency.

Letting go of overpreparation can enable a shift toward more responsive teaching. One teacher described this type of shift like this:

> Teachers like to have control… What I realized in giving up control, was that I'm giving up control to the people who deserve to have the control (the students) … Being flexible is about … having a mindset that says "I'm willing to allow my kids to explore this, because it might be better for them than what I could think of." — Eric Crouch, from *Seeing UDL in Action*
>
> (Morin, 2023)

I know that the accepted wisdom is to plan extensively and then to be willing to let go of the plan in response to how things play out in class. I also know that when I plan extensively, letting go is very difficult because I have invested so much time into my plan. In reality, the best teaching happens when we plan less, and focus on the students' responses more than on the plan.

John Hattie, in his (2003) review of research that differentiates expert teachers from experienced teachers, explained that expert teachers are more able to respond and adapt: "A key notion here is that of flexibility. Experts are more opportunistic and flexible in their teaching. They take advantage of new information, quickly bringing new interpretations and representations of the problem to light" (p. 6). Hattie also noted that expert teachers are better at improvising in response to problems, feedback, and student responses. Similarly, Berliner (2008), in an extensive study of expert teachers, noticed that expert teachers are more opportunistic and flexible in their teaching than are novices.

Livingston and Borko (1990) did a deep comparison of expert teachers with novice teachers. They found that the novices prepared more extensively than experts. They also found that experts more skillfully improvised activities and explanations around student questions and comments. None of the experts in their study had written lesson plans, but all could easily describe their mental plans for the lesson. These mental plans did not include details such as timing, pacing, or the exact number of examples and problems. Well, yes, you may say, more experienced teachers don't ***have*** to plan to the extent that beginners do. They have experience to back them up. True. But – could it be that not committing to a detailed plan freed the expert teachers up to be more responsive to students?

Lee Shulman, from Stanford University, created an in-depth portrayal of expert teaching (1987) that speaks to this idea. He compared expert teachers' flexibility and responsivity to the work of an orchestral conductor:

> (The expert teacher's) pattern of instruction, her style of teaching, is not uniform or predictable … She flexibly responds to the difficulty and character of the subject matter, the capacities of the students (which can change over the span of a single course), and her educational purposes. She can not only conduct her orchestra from the podium, she can sit back and watch it play with virtuosity itself.
>
> (Shulman, 1987, p. 3)

Shulman observed that it was flexibility, not merely the knowledge of and experience with possible scenarios, that made the difference. As an orchestral conductor myself, I've found that an ability to "be in the moment," as an entirely responsive leader, translates beautifully to classroom teaching.

Look, I'm not advocating that you not plan. Far from it. I'm suggesting that if you plan ***too*** much, it can get in the way of your ability to follow student cues, student interests, and student responses. Teachers who *over*prepare are typically unaware of the effect this has on their practice. Also, they are more at risk of burnout.

Is overpreparation a Blindspot for you? Could you be a more effective teacher if you

a) allowed the lesson to flow a little more naturally, following students' interests, questions, and choices rather than your detailed plan, and
b) were less exhausted from the hours it takes to prepare such a detailed level of planning?

Or perhaps you don't prepare enough (see Blindspot #6). Either way, Part II of this book provides strategies for you to uncover your personal Blindspot. Part III will help you address your Blindspot once you have found it.

5 Get Organized: Provide Students with Clarity, Consistency, and Accountability

While overpreparation constrains your ability to respond in the moment, a lack of organization will make instruction feel chaotic. Students depend on teachers to lead as well as to respond. Students count on teachers to provide structure with some flexibility built in.

Organizational challenges associated with Blindspot #6 result in the following:

- Students lacking clarity about what expectations are and when things will happen;
- Students lacking clarity around what they are learning and how the unit or lesson will unfold;

- Students not getting work back from grading in a timely manner;
- Students not understanding how they will be assessed and how their grades will be determined.

A teacher with this Blindspot may lack systems and routines. Planning ahead may not come naturally, so they may need to dedicate more time preparing for the day's work. They may need to develop practices like calendar use, setting aside a regular time for marking, and developing habits of regular and consistent communication with students and parents, even when that is not their most comfortable mode of operating.

A teacher could be overprepared in some ways (Blindspot #4) and still fail to provide students with clarity, consistency, and accountability. For example, a teacher who spends all their time preparing PowerPoint slides, worksheets, and highly detailed lesson plans may come up short on time they need for marking. They might overlook communicating important information about success criteria for assignments. Their students might be uncertain about when assessments are due and what consequences they face if they don't meet those deadlines – despite the more-than-adequate prep time the teacher puts into other areas.

Blindspot #5 occurs when a lack of foresight hinders clarity.

In Hattie's Visible Learning research, the factor that comes closest to "teacher organization" is "teacher clarity." Here is Hattie's Visible Learning definition of teacher clarity:

> Teacher clarity relates to organization, explanation, examples and guided practice, and assessment of student learning. It can involve clearly communicating the intentions of the lessons and the success criteria. Clear learning intentions describe the skills, knowledge, attitudes, and values that the student needs to learn.
>
> (Visible Learning – Teacher Clarity Details, n.d.)

According to Hattie's Visible Learning, teacher clarity has an effect size of 0.85 (Hattie, 2023), which is well above the "hinge point" of 0.4, and has "potential to considerably accelerate." In other words, this factor clearly has a significant impact on teaching.

If this is your Blindspot, you are in good company. Many of us struggle with this – and as a result, there are tons of resources available: lots of tools for your toolbox, plenty of podcasts, books, courses, tips, and tricks to help with teacher organization. The good news is that when you put your energy into creating systems and routines, your students will benefit tremendously. Part III of this book will help you to level up your game in this area and will direct you to resources to get you started.

6 Use Every Minute: Stop Wasting Time

Doug Lemov, in his lifelong pursuit to understand what works in classrooms, has observed hundreds of high-performing teachers. "I wanted to know not what made a teacher pretty good but what made her exceptional, able to beat the odds, what made certain teachers able to achieve what a thousand well-intentioned social programs could not" (Lemov, 2015, p. 3). Lemov's research revealed that while there were vast differences between exceptional teachers in demeanor and style, they tended to use a common set of "tools" or teaching strategies. He published these "tools" in *Teach Like a Champion*, a book I highly recommend (with the caveat to keep Blindspot #2 in the side mirror). A theme that runs through Lemov's book is efficient time use.

Lemov found that exceptional teachers honor their students' time. As such, many of the *Teach Like a Champion* strategies help to ensure that every minute of class time is spent productively. For example, Lemov explains that investing an hour to train students to pass out papers efficiently saves 3800 minutes (more than 63 hours) of additional teaching time over the course of a school year (Lemov, 2015, p. 11). Although Lemov admits that many of these strategies are uninspired and boring, they are effective, resulting in learning gains due to increased learning time. Using every minute efficiently equates to more student learning. It's as simple as that.

Blindspot #6 occurs when students sense you are wasting their time. My training as an orchestral conductor was largely focused on efficient time use. Since every musician in the room is paid union fees, every minute literally equates to dollars spent. Rehearsals start exactly on time, and end exactly on time, or else the union rep will come looking for overtime payments. As a result, every directive from the conductor needs to be precise and concise. Every moment counts.

When I transitioned to teaching school music ensembles, I found that these principles applied doubly: I couldn't afford to waste a minute of student attention, because student attention, once lost, wanders. I focused on keeping every student occupied in active learning for every possible second in class – whether this was a kindergarten music class or a high school concert band. I learned to squeeze the juice out of every moment of class time.

This principle applies to non-music classrooms as well. Teachers addressing this Blindspot can level up their game by focusing on things like

- Ensuring students know exactly what they should be doing as soon as they walk into the room, so that they don't waste time aimlessly milling about;
- Training students in efficient ways to conduct classroom tasks (such as Doug Lemov's [2021] paper-passing routines);
- Being more concise and precise in delivering instructions – as opposed to giving long explanations;
- Providing simple, clear written instructions to accompany verbal instructions;
- Setting up the physical layout of the classroom to allow for efficient transitions into and out of class and between activities (e.g., layout of desks/tables, location of student supplies).

These, and other techniques, are more fully explained in Part III of this book. Could you be using your students' time more efficiently? Are you losing precious moments of learning time? Part II of this book will help you to identify and prioritize your particular Blindspot in a way that will let you focus your energy.

7 Set Boundaries: Students Need a Teacher, not a BFF

Compared to school a generation or two ago, there is far more emphasis now on teachers being close advisors and mentors to students (Bernstein-Yamashiro & Noam, 2013). This shift in educational priorities has led teachers to focus more on building rapport with students. We work hard to make personal connections and to express interest, caring, and kindness – and we should: positive relationships between youth and adults are "the single most important ingredient in promoting positive youth development" (Pianta & Allen, 2008, p. 24).

However, teachers who desire to be a close advisor or mentor to students sometimes lose sight of professional boundaries. Time and time again, I have seen teachers overstepping in an attempt to connect with students on *their* level – as friends – and then struggle to establish respect and order in the classroom. Teachers who want to be liked more as a friend than as a teacher sometimes resort to behaviors that erode their credibility. These behaviors can include the following:

- Using slang or popular expressions;
- Employing "Kidspeak" or mimicking students' vocal inflections (see Blindspot #3);
- Engaging in friendly banter with some (but not all) of the students;
- Over-sharing their personal details – sometimes with the hope that this will encourage students to disclose their own;
- Trying to be cool;
- Employing an inconsistent classroom management style;
- Being over-interested in students' personal or emotional lives, to the point where students feel awkward.

Ken Braddy, in his (2018) blog post, addressed this topic as he reflected on his early teaching days:

> We probably crossed the line a time or two as young, inexperienced teachers, wanting the kids to like us to the point that we strayed into "BFF territory." … Be the adult,

> not the BFF, and keep a firm hand on the relationship wheel. The students you lead need just that – a leader – not a best friend. They have plenty of those.
>
> (Braddy, 2018)

The reality is, we go into this profession because we like kids. We want to make a real difference in our students' lives. We are kind, empathetic, and caring people. We naturally want to be liked by the people we care so much about. No wonder this Blindspot occurs so frequently!

Hattie's Visible Learning research shows that "teacher credibility" has a 1.09 effect size (Hattie, 2023). This is significant, compared to the "hinge point" of 0.4, meaning it has potential to considerably accelerate learning.

Blindspot #7 occurs when familiarity overrides leadership.
Because "teacher credibility" is undermined when a teacher oversteps professional boundaries, this Blindspot is important. Try too hard to be liked, and you lose that important ingredient that allows you to be the teacher, allows you to do your job, and gives the students reason to respect you.

Are you over-focused on your personal relationships with students? How important is it that your students like you? How much do you want to be "their person"? Do you secretly want to be the "cool teacher," the popular one with the kids?

Having a warm, professional rapport with your students is critically important; however, desiring their friendship, or wanting to be their "trusted adult" (rather than desiring *that they have* a trusted adult), is a red flag. Your honest answers to these questions will help you identify whether this is a Blindspot for you.

8 Move the Bar: Set an Appropriate Level of Challenge

Are you aiming too high? Too low? Get it wrong, and your students will feel bored and patronized – or frustrated and inept. Or both.

Let's start with setting the bar too low. Back in 1964, Harvard psychologist Robert Rosenthal created an experiment to determine whether teachers' expectations of their students become self-fulfilling prophecies. The results were the now-famous *Pygmalion in the Classroom* (Rosenthal & Jacobson, 1968), a study which led to an avalanche of research on what academics call "teacher expectations."

Rosenthal conducted the study at Spruce Elementary school in San Francisco, in collaboration with the school's principal, Lenore Jacobson. After administering an IQ test to all the students, the researchers told the teachers that small groups of children in each classroom were poised to "bloom" academically (Ellison, 2015). It turned out that over the next year, these children did just that: the ones labeled as gifted excelled academically compared to their peers. The younger students in particular showed dramatically increased IQ scores at the end of the year.

Because the "gifted" children had been randomly selected, their gains could only have been caused by their teachers' belief in their potential. According to Rosenthal: "If we expect certain behaviors from people, we treat them differently — and that treatment is likely to affect their behavior" (Ellison, 2015).

Researcher Christine Rubie-Davies subsequently made a career of understanding the effect of teacher expectations. Her research (2015, 2016) supports the idea that teachers with high expectations (compared to teachers with grade-level or low expectations)

- spend more time providing a framework for students' learning,
- provide their students with more feedback,
- question their students using more higher-order questions,
- manage their students' behavior more positively,
- give more class-level feedback, and
- are more likely to question further and provide explanations when a student gives a correct answer.

Blindspot #8 occurs when expectations don't align with student ability.

John Hattie (2003) explained:

> Expert teachers [compared to experienced teachers] provide appropriately challenging tasks and goals for students. Expert teachers are more likely to set challenging rather than 'do your best' goals, they set challenging and not merely time-consuming activities, they invite students to engage rather than copy, and they aim to encourage students to share commitment to these challenging goals.
>
> (p. 9)

Note Hattie's words above: *appropriately challenging*. While teachers need to set high expectations for their students, setting learning goals too high can lead to student distress and frustration. Hattie calls this "the Goldilocks's principle of challenge: not too hard, not too easy, and not too boring" (visiblelearningmetax.com). I have observed teachers who operate with a constructivist mindset set tasks that have left students feeling bewildered. We want our students to struggle, to grapple with material, to figure things out themselves – but too little scaffolding results in floundering.

The first year that I taught high-school-level Economics, I asked my grade 11 economics students to engage in a discussion applying the concept of dialectical materialism to the ideas of Karl Marx and Adam Smith. We went through the readings, watched some helpful videos, and launched into a discussion. I realized right away that the students did not have a grasp of the underlying concepts. They struggled to find things to say, then too quickly rallied around oversimplified ideas (e.g., "communism doesn't work" and "capitalism is bad"). These students needed much more support in understanding the underlying concepts before they could engage in a productive discussion. I had pitched that bar too high, too early, and they were left with unsupported beliefs based on insufficient reasoning. (We spent a few more classes reviewing the subject matter so that the students could then engage in well-supported discussion.)

Gravois and Gickling (2002) defined appropriate instructional level as "a comfort zone created when the student has sufficient prior knowledge and skill to successfully interact with the task and still learn new information" (p. 888). Research has consistently shown that teaching children at their individual instructional level results in increased student learning (Burns & Dean, 2002, Burns, 2004; Gickling & Rosenfield, 1995; Shapiro, 1992; Tomlinson & Kalbfleisch, 1998). In his Visible Learning research, Hattie showed that the effect size for "appropriately challenging goals" is 0.59, well above the 0.4 hinge-point, and thus has "potential to considerably accelerate learning."

An interesting piece of research by Gentry et al. (2002) suggests that the level of instructional challenge is frequently outside of teachers' awareness. These researchers examined 91 elementary and 64 middle school classes and found that there was no relationship between the level of challenge that teachers reported and the level of challenge that students perceived. In other words, what teachers reported was not what students actually experienced. Clearly, this was a Blindspot for the 154 teachers in the study.

Hitting that sweet spot – that Goldilocks zone – can make a significant impact on student learning. Is this an area of focus you need to address? Part II of this book will help you discern if this is an important issue for you. Part III will give you tools and strategies to help you address it.

9 Make It Safe to Make Mistakes: Create a Positive "Error Culture"

We all know that learning takes place in psychologically safe spaces where students feel that errors are welcomed, where they can learn from their mistakes, and where they can feel comfortable asking questions. Particularly as we embrace constructivist models of teaching and learning, students must feel safe to explore, to experiment, and to deal with errors.

Research shows that teachers' everyday behaviors have a substantial impact on students' attitudes toward mistakes. Tulis (2013) collected data from 685 grade 5 students in 25 different classes and observed their teachers in action. The researchers coded teacher responses to students' mistakes and found that the most common teacher response was the classic "Bermuda triangle of error correction" – where teachers redirect an incorrectly answered question to another student. One of the most common strategies, this is observed more than 30% of the time in U.S. schools (Santagata 2005) and is associated with students feeling unsafe and error-avoidant. Other maladaptive responses to mistakes included the teacher simply correcting the student's mistake, stating "no, that is not correct," or displaying a negative facial affect (shaking the head, frowning, etc.). Adaptive responses to mistakes included praising the student's thought or approach, praising the student's active contribution, and emphasizing the learning potential of the mistake.

Tulis (2013) then compared observed teacher behaviors to students' responses to questions, like "I am often afraid of making mistakes in this class" and "I feel embarrassed when I make an error in class." Students in classes where teacher behaviors were adaptive to mistakes were more likely to exhibit positive attitudes toward learning and school, and toward making errors. Furthermore, Steuer and Dresel (2015) demonstrated that positive error climates are associated with academic achievement.

Hattie's (2003) research confirmed that expert teachers (compared to experienced teachers) build classroom climates where errors are welcomed and where student questioning is high: in other words, expert teachers create a positive "error culture." Clearly, this is an important aspect of teaching, and one we all need to constantly address.

Blindspot #9 occurs when students are wary of making mistakes.

I don't believe there is a teacher on the planet who is ***not*** aware of the importance of students' attitudes toward experimenting, taking risks, making errors, and learning from mistakes. Most of us would strongly assert that we create a positive error culture in our classrooms!

But how do you know? What do your students actually experience?

Teachers I have worked with on Blindspot #9 are always dubious at the start. They resist the idea that students are afraid to make mistakes in their classes. They have a hard time accepting that students worry about appearing stupid. They are unaware of the impact of their tone of voice, their choice of words, and their facial expressions in response to students' attempts, mistakes, and failures as well as to students' successes.

The good news is that this can be a fairly straightforward Blindspot to address, once you are aware of it. There are lots of strategies available to help teachers create a supportive, risk-embracing, and error-tolerant classroom climate. Part II of this book will help you to identify whether this is a priority for your practice, and Part III of this book will show you how to address this Blindspot.

10 Like Them All: Show Students You're on Their Side

One of the teachers I admire most, one whose grade 4 classroom is a beautiful learning community, is also one of the clearest thinkers I know. In response to my admiration of his work, he said simply: "I just try to like them all. Some of them are pretty hard to like, but I do my best." The work he does in this classroom is profoundly complex, strategic, and nuanced. His students' learning outcomes are superb. And his interactions with every one of his students are consistently respectful and affirming. Yet his mantra is so simple. This idea: "try to like them all" focuses his energy, so that at the end of the day, regardless of whatever ups or downs they may have had, every one of his students feels whole.

I have spoken to many, many students who believe that they have a teacher who doesn't like them. And yet I don't believe there is a teacher in existence who will admit to not liking a student. Nor have I ever heard a teacher acknowledge that they have students who ***know*** they don't like them. A frequent scenario is this: the teacher believes that they are firm, fair, kind, and warm to all their students; meanwhile, if you ask the students, some – or all of them – perceive being disliked.

To compound the issue, students don't typically make their feelings about being disliked evident. For example, Wells (1996), in a classic study of classroom climate, described such a situation:

> Students' frustrations were largely hidden under a cover of politeness and acquiescence. For instance, even though the students from Meadowbrook alternately despised, feared, and tolerated [one of their teachers] and didn't believe they were learning that much—they didn't directly challenge him. They understood that it would make no difference, except perhaps to make things worse.
>
> (p. 133)

If students in your class generally felt disliked, they would not likely tell you. You would really have no way of knowing.

Blindspot #10 occurs when there is a lack of respect, regard, and support for all students equally.

Most often, it is not the entire class, but one or two students who carry a sense that the teacher "has it out for them." Typically, these are the students who demonstrate unlikeable behaviors – acting out, seeking attention, breaking the rules, and so on – and as a result, they receive frequent negative feedback from the teacher. Unfortunately, research shows that students who feel disliked by their teacher are disproportionately from a racial minority (Tenenbaum & Ruck, 2007) physically unattractive (Ritts et al., 1992; Shaw, 2001) or have learning disabilities (Murray & Greenberg, 2001).

Feeling liked by your teacher is profoundly important. Don't get me wrong – not liked in a peer-to-peer sense as a friend (see Blindspot #5), but as in feeling a positive regard from the teacher. Research shows that "students perceiving that they are not liked by the teacher" is strongly associated with poor academic performance (e.g., Roorda et al., 2011; McGrath & Van Bergen, 2015), while students who perceived their teachers to be supportive report enhanced motivation and agency (Cohen et al., 2020) and receive higher grades (Davis, 2003). Non-academic outcomes, such as behavioral problems and poor long-term social adjustment, also result when students feel disliked by their teacher (e.g., Decker et al., 2007, Furrer & Skinner, 2003). For example, a long-term study showed that kindergarten students who felt disliked by their teacher exhibited poor academic and social outcomes through to middle and high school (Card, 2010).

Research on students' perceptions of their teacher is limited; however, one study stands out: Raufelder et al. (2016) spoke with 86 grade 7 and 8 students to try to understand how students perceive "good" and "bad" teachers, based on their daily school experiences. Almost all of the students talked extensively about their desire to be appreciated by their teacher. The most common trait of "bad" teachers? Aggression (yelling, being angry). Students also spoke about preferential treatment of individuals or groups of students – for example: "He [the teacher] has his favorite students, so that naturally drives me crazy" (p. 37). The researchers concluded that when evaluating the effectiveness of a teacher, most students valued personal qualities above professional skills (such as content knowledge and pedagogical expertise) and that at the end of the day, most students just wanted to be liked by their teacher.

The reality is, not all students are easy to like. I know it. There are behaviors that make it challenging at times to maintain a positive regard. However, research shows that students are highly attuned to sensing teachers' feelings for them (e.g., Babad, 1995; Kuklinski & Weinstein, 2000). It is vitally important to maintain a high level of self-awareness in this regard. Like the fourth-grade teacher I described at the beginning of this section, the self-aware teacher needs to focus on maintaining a positive regard for every child in the room and ensuring that every child receives equal warmth, empathy, and appreciation.

This Blindspot is about the quality of the relationship you have with every one of your students. Because your students will probably not volunteer how they perceive you or feel about you, this Blindspot is especially difficult to identify. The next section offers several strategies to help you identify if this is the Blindspot most impacting your effectiveness.

Why These Ten?

In curating the ten Classic Blindspots, I returned again and again to my driving question: of all the infinitely many things that trip us up as teachers, of all the things that need attending to, which are the most important in terms of (a) prevalence in teacher practice and (b) impact on student learning? Reflecting on 25 years of professional practice and my work with hundreds of teachers, I know any teacher would benefit from addressing their own Blindspot from these Classic Ten Blindspots– including myself!

The list is simple and obvious. The challenge is in discovering which one most applies to you.

How does this list compare to teacher-development priorities identified in the research literature? Surprisingly, while there is a great deal of research that documents what teachers do well, there is very little research that identifies prevalent teacher weaknesses. Consider teacher evaluation models. The best ones are based on a solid foundation of research. However, because their purpose is evaluation as well as development, they have to focus on all aspects of professional competency. This means they contain a complete and exhaustive set of all the factors that characterize excellence in teaching. The Marzano et al. (2013) teacher evaluation model contains 65 components. Similarly, the Charlotte Danielson Framework for Teaching (FFT) contains six "clusters," 22 components, and 76 elements. Necessary for teacher evaluation? Absolutely. As a tool for raising self-awareness? Too much.

Most of us have a pretty good handle on most of the components in these teacher evaluation models – things like "planning and preparing for use of available materials for upcoming units and lessons" (domain 2, element 4 from Marzano's model). But to raise teachers' awareness about addressing their "lowest-hanging-fruit," I wanted research that directly identified aspects of teaching that commonly go awry.

I did eventually find some literature that honed in on the specifics that commonly trip us up: first, Akita and Sakamoto's (2014) study of professional development in Japan. These researchers simplified the Pro-D process into a set of questions that they advised teachers to reflect on every year:

1. Does the teacher talk too much?
2. Does the teacher repeat the same explanations again and again?
3. Is the level of learning in the task too easy for students?
4. Do teachers set small steps for success and deprive children of their ability to think and enquire?

5. Is the learning task just a game of guessing the correct answer that the teacher sets in advance?
6. Does the teacher fully use the children's creative ideas to help everyone understand the lesson?
7. Is the vision of how children develop through this unit clear for the teacher and the children?

(p. 39)

These align nicely with the Classic Ten Blindspots:

- Points 1 and 2 – "Does the teacher talk too much?" and "Does the teacher repeat the same explanations again and again?" are essentially Blindspot 1 (Cut the words).
- Point 3 – "Is the level of learning in the task too easy for students?" relates to setting an appropriate level of challenge, which is Blindspot 8 (Move the bar).
- Points 4 and 5 – "Do teachers set small steps for success and deprive children of their ability to think and enquire?" and "Is the learning task just a game of guessing the correct answer that the teacher sets in advance?" combine Blindspot 8 (Move the bar) and Blindspot 3 (Loosen the reins).
- Point 6 – "Does the teacher fully use the children's creative ideas to help everyone understand the lesson?" relates to Blindspot 3 (Loosen the reigns) and Blindspot 4 (Check overpreparation): a teacher who is tightly controlled and overly pre-planned may be less likely to follow the students' lead and allow student ideas to carry the lesson.
- Point 7 – "Is the vision of how children develop through this unit clear for the teacher and the children?" relates to Blindspot 5 (Get organized).

However, Akita and Sakamoto's seven questions don't address Blindspots 2, 4, 7, 9, or 10.

In a research paper refreshingly titled "What you don't know can hurt you: Students' perceptions of professors' annoying teaching habits," researchers Miley and Gonsalves (2003) found that university professors are unaware of the teaching behaviors that are most annoying to students. The researchers' method was simple: they handed out index cards to 874 undergraduate students and asked that they write down (anonymously) "at least one thing about previous professors (at your current school or elsewhere) that you find inhibited your learning, was annoying, or was frustrating" (p. 449). The results revealed the most common to be: disorganized teaching (Blindspot 5 – Get organized), talking too fast for students to process information (Blindspot 2 – Fix verbal hazards), lecturing in a monotone voice (Blindspot 2 – Fix verbal hazards), and degrading students (Blindspot 10 – Like them all).

From observation, research, and my work coaching the teachers I know – including myself! – to become ever better, I know that the Classic 10 Blindspots trip up teachers in every kind of learning environment. I also know that awareness, prioritization, and self-improvement will show immediate benefits in your classroom, in your enjoyment of teaching, and in your relationship with every one of your students.

Are there other aspects of teaching that can significantly impact student learning in your classroom? Absolutely. Use of sound assessment methods comes to mind. Read a book by Tom Schimmer or Tom Guskey and you will know whether or not you have work to do in that department. Your personal Blindspot from the Classic Ten, however, will remain hidden from you until you raise your self-awareness.

I know which one is my Blindspot – or it *was* a Blindspot until I became aware of it. Which one is yours? Part II of this book will help you determine which one of these is most impacting your practice and which one, if addressed, will make the biggest difference to your students' experience in your classroom.

References

Akita, K., & Sakamoto, A. (2014). Lesson study and teachers' professional development in Japan. In *Realising Learning* (pp. 41–56). Routledge.

Assor, A., & Kaplan, H. (2001). Mapping the domain of autonomy support: Five important ways to enhance or undermine student's experience of autonomy in learning. In A. Efklides, J. Kuhl, & R. M. Sorrentino

(Eds.), *Trends and prospects in motivation research* (pp. 101–120). Dordrecht, The Netherlands: Kluwer.

Assor, A., Kaplan, H., Kanat-Maymon, Y., & Roth, G. (2005). Directly controlling teacher behaviors as predictors of poor motivation and engagement in girls and boys: The role of anger and anxiety. *Learning and Instruction*, *15*(5), 397–413.

Assor, A., Kaplan, H., & Roth, G. (2002). Choice is good, but relevance is excellent: autonomy-enhancing and suppressing teacher behaviors predicting students' engagement in schoolwork. *British Journal of Educational Psychology*, *72*, 261e278.

Babad, E. (1995). The "teacher's pet" phenomenon, students' perceptions of teachers' differential behavior, and students' morale. *Journal of Educational Psychology*, *87*(3), 361–374. https://doi.org/10.1037/0022-0663.87.3.361

Berliner, D. C. (2008). The nature of expertise in teaching. In M. Cochran-Smith, S. Feiman-Nemser, D. J. McIntyre, & K. E. Demers (Eds.), *Handbook of research on teacher education* (3rd ed., pp. 808–823). Routledge.

Bernstein-Yamashiro, B., & Noam, G. G. (2013). Establishing and maintaining boundaries in teacher-student relationships. *New Directions for Youth Development*, *2013*(137), 69–84.

Braddy, V. a. P. B. K., Jr. (2018, August 7). *Tuesday teaching tip: Be the adult, not their BFF*. kenbraddy.com. https://kenbraddy.com/2018/08/07/tuesday-teaching-tip-be-the-adult-not-their-bff/

Burns, M. K. (2004). Empirical analysis of drill ratio research: Refining the instructional level for drill tasks. *Remedial and Special Education*, *25*(3), 167–173.

Burns, M. K., & Dean, V. J. (2002). Rethinking the instructional level: Impact on assessment and intervention. In *annual conference of the National Association of School Psychologists*, Chicago, IL.

Card, N. A. (2010). Antipathetic relationships in child and adolescent development: A meta-analytic review and recommendations for an emerging area of study. *Developmental Psychology*, *46*(2), 516–529. https://doi.org/10.1037/a0017199

Cohen, R., Moed, A., Shoshani, A., Roth, G., & Kanat-Maymon, Y. (2020). Teachers' conditional regard and students' need satisfaction and agentic engagement: A multilevel motivation mediation model. *Journal of Youth and Adolescence*, *49*, 790–803.

Davis, H. A. (2003). Conceptualizing the role of student–teacher relationships on children's social and cognitive development. *Educational Psychologist*, *38*, 207–234. 123 426

De Alvear, R. M. B., Barón, F. J., & Martínez-Arquero, A. G. (2011). School teachers' vocal use, risk factors, and voice disorder prevalence: Guidelines to detect teachers with current voice problems. *Folia Phoniatrica et Logopaedica*, *63*(4), 209–215.

De Brito Mota, A. F., Giannini, S. P. P., de Oliveira, I. B., Paparelli, R., Dornelas, R., & Ferreira, L. P. (2019). Voice disorder and burnout syndrome in teachers. *Journal of Voice*, *33*(4), 581–e7.

Decker, D. M., Dona, D. P., & Christenson, S. L. (2007). Behaviorally at-risk African American students: The importance of student–teacher relationships for student outcomes. *Journal of School Psychology*, *45*(1), 83–109.

Edwards, S. (2024, May 8). *Professional Development Courses for Teachers - Teacher Webinar*. Danielson Group. https://danielsongroup.org/the-framework-for-teaching/

Ellison, K. (2015). Being honest about the Pygmalion effect. *Discover Magazine*, October. 28, 2015 https://sites.tufts.edu/tuftsliteracycorps/files/2017/02/Being-Honest-About-the-Pygmalion-Effect-2015.pdf

Furrer, C. & Skinner, E. (2003). Sense of relatedness as a factor in children's academic engagement and performance. *Journal of Educational Psychology*, *95* (2003), 148–162. https://doi.org/10.1037/0022-0663.95.1.14

Gallimore, R., & Tharp, R. (2004). What a coach can teach a teacher, 1975–2004: Reflections and reanalysis of John Wooden's teaching practices. *The Sport Psychologist*, *18*(2), 119–137.

Gentry, M., Rizza, M. G., & Owen, S. V. (2002). Examining perceptions of challenge and choice in classrooms: The relationship between teachers and their students and comparisons between gifted students and other students. *The Gifted Child Quarterly*, *46*(2), 145–155.

Gharbavi, A., & Iravani, H. (2014). Is teacher talk pernicious to students? A discourse analysis of teacher talk. *Procedia-Social and Behavioral Sciences*, *98*, 552–561.

Gickling, E., & Rosenfield, S. (1995). Best practices in curriculum-based assessment. In A. Thomas & J. Grimes (Eds.), *Best practices in school psychology* (3rd ed., pp. 587–595). National Association of School Psychologists.

Gravois, T. A., & Gickling, E. E. (2002). Best practices in curriculum-based assessment. In A. Thomas & J. Grimes (Eds.), *Best practices in school psychology IV* (pp. 885–898). National Association of School Psychologists.

Hattie, J. (2003). Teachers make a difference, What is the research evidence? Paper presented at the *Building Teacher Quality: What does the research tell us? ACER Research Conference*, Melbourne, Australia.

Hattie, J. (2012). *Visible learning for teachers: Maximizing impact on learning*. Routledge.

Hattie, J. (2023). *Visible learning: The sequel*. Routledge.

Hattie, J., & Yates, G. C. (2013). *Visible learning and the science of how we learn*. Routledge.

Jang, H. (2021). How cute do I sound to you?: Gender and age effects in the use and evaluation of Korean baby-talk register, Aegyo. *Language Sciences*, *83*, 101289.

Kostadinovska-Stojchevska, B., & Popovikj, I. (2019). Teacher talking time vs. student talking time: Moving from teacher-centered classroom to learner-centered classroom. *The International Journal of Applied Language Studies and Culture*, *2*(2), 25–31.

Kuklinski, M. R., & Weinstein, R. S. (2000). Classroom and grade level differences in the stability of teacher expectations and perceived differential teacher treatment. *Learning Environments Research*, *3*(1), 1–34. https://doi.org/10.1023/A:1009904718353

Lemov, D. (2015). *Teach like a champion 2.0: 63 Techniques that put students on the path to college*. John Wiley & Sons.

Lemov, D. (2021). *Teach like a champion 3.0: 63 Techniques that put students on the path to college*. John Wiley & Sons.

Livingston, C., & Borko, H. (1990). High school mathematics review lessons: Expert-novice distinctions. *Journal for Research in Mathematics Education*, *21*(5), 372–387.

Martin, S., & Darnley, L. (2017). *The voice in education: Vocal health and effective communication*. Compton Publishing Ltd.

Martins, R. H. G., Pereira, E. R. B. N., Hidalgo, C. B., & Tavares, E. L. M. (2014). Voice disorders in teachers. A review. *Journal of voice*, *28*(6), 716–724.

Marzano, R. J., & Toth, M. D. (2013). *Teacher evaluation that makes a difference: A new model for teacher growth and student achievement*. ASCD. https://www.marzanocenter.com/wp-content/uploads/sites/4/2019/04/FTEM_Updated_Michigan_08312017.pdf

McGrath, K. F., & Van Bergen, P. (2015). Who, when, why and to what end? Students at risk of negative student–teacher relationships and their outcomes. *Educational Research Review*, *14*, 1–17.

McWhorter, J. (2019, April 19). Why do adults talk like children? *The Atlantic*. https://www.theatlantic.com/magazine/archive/2019/05/why-young-adults-are-talking-like-3-year-olds/586000/

Meador, D. (2019, May 4). *Strategies for Teachers: The power of preparation and planning*. ThoughtCo. https://www.thoughtco.com/power-of-preparation-and-planning-3194263

Miley, W. M., & Gonsalves, S. (2003). What you don't know can hurt you: Students' perceptions of professors' annoying teaching habits. *College Student Journal*, *37*(3), 44–456. https://link.gale.com/apps/doc/A108836910/AONE?u=anon~fa4c0cfb&sid=googleScholar&xid=dfa8bf47

Morin, A. (2023, November 8). *What is Universal Design for Learning (UDL)?* Understood. https://www.understood.org/en/articles/universal-design-for-learning-what-it-is-and-how-it-works

Morton, V., & Watson, D. R. (1998). The teaching voice: Problems and perceptions. *Logopedics, Phoniatrics, Vocology*, *23*, 133–139.

Murray, C., & Greenberg, M. T. (2001). Relationships with teachers and bonds with school: Social emotional adjustment correlates for children with and without disabilities. *Psychology in the Schools*, *38*(1), 25–41.

Perlman, B., & McCann, L. I. (1998). Student's pet peeves about teaching. *Teaching of Psychology*, *25*(3), 201–203.

Pianta, R. C., & Allen, J. P. (2008). *Building capacity for positive youth development in secondary school classrooms: Changing teachers' interactions with students*. APA PsycNet.

Raufelder, D., Nitsche, L., Breitmeyer, S., Keßler, S., Herrmann, E., & Regner, N. (2016). Students' perception of "good" and "bad" teachers—Results of a qualitative thematic analysis with German adolescents. *International Journal of Educational Research*, *75*, 31–44.

Reeve, J., & Cheon, S. H. (2021). Autonomy-supportive teaching: Its malleability, benefits, and potential to improve educational practice. *Educational Psychologist*, *56*(1), 54–77.

Ritts, V., Patterson, M. L., & Tubbs, M. E. (1992). Expectations, impressions, and judgments of physically attractive students: A review. *Review of Educational Research*, *62*(4), 413–426.

Roorda, D. L., Koomen, H. M., Spilt, J. L., & Oort, F. J. (2011). The influence of affective teacher–student relationships on students' school engagement and achievement: A meta-analytic approach. *Review of Educational Research*, *81*(4), 493–529.

Rosenthal, R., & Jacobson, L. (1968). Pygmalion in the classroom. *The Urban Review*, *3*(1), 16–20.

Rubie-Davies, C. M., Peterson, E. R., Sibley, C. G., & Rosenthal, R. (2015). A teacher expectation intervention: Modelling the practices of high expectation teachers. *Contemporary Educational Psychology*, *40*, 72–85. https://doi.org/10.1016/j.cedpsych.2014.03.003

Rubie-Davies, C. M., & Rosenthal, R. (2016). Intervening in teachers' expectations: A random effects meta-analytic approach to examining the effectiveness of an intervention. *Learning and Individual Differences*, *50*, 83–92. https://doi.org/10.1016/j.lindif.2016.07.014

Santagata, R. (2005). Practices and beliefs in mistake-handling activities: A video study of Italian and US mathematics lessons. *Teaching and Teacher Education*, *21*(5), 491–508.

Shapiro, E. S. (1992). Use of Gickling's model of curriculum-based assessment to improve reading in elementary age students. *School Psychology Review*, *21*, 168–176.

Shaw, W. (2001). Influence of children's physical attractiveness on teacher expectations. *The Journal of Social Psychology*, *128*(3), 373–383.

Shulman, L. S. (1987). Knowledge and teaching: Foundations of the new reform. *Harvard Educational Review*, *19*(2), 4–14.

Smith, K.S. (2019). Are you an overfunctioner? *Psychology Today* (October 17, 2019). https://www.psychologytoday.com/us/blog/everything-isnt-terrible/201910/are-you-overfunctioner

Steuer, G., & Dresel, M. (2015). A constructive error climate as an element of effective learning environments. *Psychological Test and Assessment Modeling*, *57*(2), 262.

Tenenbaum, H. R., & Ruck, M. D. (2007). Are teachers' expectations different for racial minority than for European American students? A meta-analysis. *Journal of Educational Psychology, 99*(2), 253–273. https://doi.org/10.1037/0022-0663.99.2.253

Tomlinson, C. A., & Kalbfleisch, M. L. (1998). Teach me, teach my brain: A call for differentiated classrooms. *Educational Leadership, 56*(3), 50–55.

Tulis, M. (2013). Error management behavior in classrooms: Teachers' responses to student mistakes. *Teaching and Teacher Education, 33*, 56–68. https://doi.org/10.1016/j.tate.2013.02.003

Tyler, J. C. (2015). Expanding and mapping the indexical field: Rising pitch, the uptalk stereotype, and perceptual variation. *Journal of English Linguistics, 43*(4), 284–310.

Van Houtte, E., Claeys, S., Wuyts, F., & Van Lierde, K. (2011). The impact of voice disorders among teachers: Vocal complaints, treatment-seeking behavior, knowledge of vocal care, and voice-related absenteeism. *Journal of Voice, 25*(5), 570–575.

Vansteenkiste, M., Aelterman, N., Haerens, L., & Soenens, B. (2019). Seeking stability in stormy educational times: A need-based perspective on (de)motivating teaching grounded in self-determination theory. In E. N. Gonida & M. S. Lemos (Eds.), *Motivation in education at a time of global change: Theory, research, and implications for practice* (Vol. 20, pp. 53–80). Emerald.

Visible Learning - Teacher clarity Details. (n.d.). https://www.visiblelearningmetax.com/influences/view/teacher_clarity

Visible Learning Meta[x]. website: https://www.visiblelearningmetax.com/

Waring, H. Z. (2021). Harnessing the power of heteroglossia: How to multitask with teacher talk. *Classroom-based conversation analytic research: Theoretical and applied perspectives on pedagogy* (pp. 281–301). Springer.

Warren, P. (2016). *Uptalk: The phenomenon of rising intonation*. Cambridge University Press.

Wells, M. C. (1996). *Literacies lost: When students move from a progressive middle school to a traditional high school*. Teachers College Press.

White, D. (2019, October 6). *The basics are how it's done - Dana K. White: A slob comes clean*. Dana K. White: A Slob Comes Clean. https://www.aslobcomesclean.com/2012/02/the-basics-are-how-its-done-for-everyone/

Part II

Six Strategies to Help You Find Your Blindspot

3

Before You Start, Adopt a Feedback Mindset

> Most advice, no matter how it is framed, runs a significant risk of being ignored. — Forsythe and Johnson (2017)

The work of finding your Blindspot begins with raising your self-awareness. This means letting go of the schema you have developed about yourself (e.g., I'm a great teacher, my students love me, I'm really good at classroom management) and being open to the possibility that something else may be true. It means questioning your currently held beliefs and seeking evidence that may confirm or disconfirm those beliefs. It means opening yourself up, being vulnerable, and letting go of defenses, resistance, and judgment. Your ego will have to take a step back and sit in the passenger's seat. Easy to say, hard to do.

We all have schema about ourselves and about others. Creating schema is the ego's way of making sense of the world. I had a schema about an administrator I worked under, to try to explain her chilly interactions with me – my schema that she was insecure worked pretty well and helped me to deflect her unfriendliness. I may have been incorrect – she may or may not have been insecure – but my schema helped me make sense of some otherwise off-putting behaviors. I also have schemas about myself: I am mostly a terrific mum, a not-so-good cook, a so-so

DOI: 10.4324/9781003490975-6

piano player, and a good teacher. This last schema is the one that gets in the way of my professional development.

When the schema of ourselves as a "good teacher" tries to exist alongside inferences or evidence that we are not, the result is discomfort: anxiety, anger, and emotional distress. This discomfort, called *cognitive dissonance*, is a very human response. And an equally human response, in order to preserve our schema and alleviate the discomfort, is to ignore or dismiss any evidence to the contrary. Hence the quote at the top of this chapter.

Sorry to say, if we want to raise our self-awareness, we don't get to take the easy option of ignoring or discounting the evidence. We don't get to "blame it on the kids." (Oh well, that group is just out of control. Those kids haven't had the right support at home. They're not interested in learning. Etc., etc.) We don't get to say that an incident was a one-off. (That person doesn't know what they're talking about.) Nope. All of it counts.

If we want to raise our self-awareness, we will have to look at all the evidence we can find squarely in the face and give it its day in court. We will have to regard any and all feedback, data, inferences, etc. as valuable gold: seize it, covet it, take it to the bank. All of it can help us identify patterns and trends, which will help us get to the truth. The correct response can only ever be an enthusiastic "Thanks for the feedback!"

Meanwhile, we must lay aside schema about being a "good teacher." Finding your Blindspot is not about being "good" or "bad." It's about being *better*. Better tomorrow than we are today. Better next month than we are this month. So just step off that train. Tell your schema to go have a cup of coffee while we get to work.

This requires humility. Humility is being open to the idea that we are not perfect and that we have much to learn. But remember that humility is "the mid-point between the two negative extremes of arrogance and lack of self-esteem" (Vera & Rodriguez-Lopez, 2004, p. 395). We're not talking about self-effacement, abasement, or humiliation. We're talking about healthy humility, which simply means freedom from pride or arrogance. It requires toughness and emotional resilience (Coulehan, 2010, p. 200) as well as kindness to oneself and others.

The best path to self-awareness is to embrace a "we" mindset. We are all on a learning journey. We all desire to give our students the best we can. It is completely irrelevant who is or who is not a "good" teacher (unless you are an administrator with hiring and firing responsibilities – but, then, this book is not for you). If you can acknowledge that we *all* have a Blindspot and that you are ready and willing to find yours, address it, and do better for your students, then you have taken the first step to adopting a feedback mindset.

Once you have adopted a feedback mindset, you will be able to benefit from the "tough love" approach that I take in this book. Your teaching is important. Your students are important. You deserve no-nonsense, to-the-point guidance to doing better.

At the same time, give yourself – with all your flaws, beauty spots, quirks, and imperfections – some grace. You are who you are. We all start somewhere. You have come a long way in your teaching practice already, and opportunities for improvement abound. Self-compassion combined with humility is a powerful combination. Adopt a feedback mindset and shower yourself and others with compassion – and you have set the stage for tremendous professional growth.

References

Coulehan, J. (2010). On humility. *Annals of Internal Medicine*, *153*(3), 200–201.

Forsythe, A., & Johnson, S. (2017). Thanks, but no thanks for the feedback. *Assessment & Evaluation in Higher Education*, *42*(6), 850–859.

Vera, D. & Rodriguez-Lopez, A. (2004). Strategic virtues: Humility as a source of competitive advantage. *Organizational Dynamics* *33*(4), 393–408.

4

Flip the Coin

> Through pride we are ever deceiving ourselves. — Attributed to Carl Jung

A long time ago, I had an administrator who gave me some great advice that has stuck with me ever since. I was in her office, having my annual review. The review process at that particular school consisted of my going through a fairly exhaustive self-evaluation checklist, going over my filled-out self-evaluation with her, and then talking through my plans for professional growth.

Having been on the other side of the evaluation desk many a time, I had experienced the shortcomings of the self-evaluation process firsthand. I had worked, time and time again, with staff who did *not* bring up the one thing that glaringly needed addressing. A teacher who talked down to her students with a tone of voice better suited to much younger children would propose to work on problem-based learning. A teacher who had classroom management issues would choose a goal of creating better rubrics for assessment. A teacher who was prone to lecturing students to the point where they disengaged would identify curriculum documentation as the primary focus for their teacher development. This inability to identify the most important weaknesses in our own teaching seemed ubiquitous. And it made complete sense to me: if they knew the thing that really needed fixing, they would have fixed it already.

DOI: 10.4324/9781003490975-7

So there I was, sitting in Lois's office, telling her that I thought I would work on my assessment practices, while this voice in my head kept saying "There's probably something else, something more important, something you really need to address, something that she is dying to tell you straight out, but can't, because this is meant to be a self-evaluation based growth model." The most she could do was to gently coach me toward discovering my weak area for myself – but what were the chances? She was a busy administrator. Each professional growth meeting was scheduled for half an hour. It takes much more time than that to gently coach someone to discover something outside of their awareness.

So I cut to the chase and asked her straight out: "What is my Blindspot? What am I not seeing? What is the number one adjustment I need to make in my teaching?"

Lois thought for a moment. And then she said a very wise thing: "Everybody's strength has a flip side, which can be their biggest weakness. It's like two sides of a coin: the trait that is your biggest strength can also be the one that trips you up." I nodded, hoping she would say more. She did: "In your case," she continued, "it's your nimbleness. You think quickly, you move quickly, you're very flexible and able to respond to things in a flash. This is a great quality: it means you have great ideas, and you can implement them right away."

This was true. I do move quickly. I love being flexible, responding to the moment, seeing a need in real-time and adjusting to meet it. I nodded, hoping she would explain the flip side of this trait – I mean, flexibility, responsiveness – those are good things, right?

She continued. The flip side is that you move before other people are ready, and this throws them off. Not everyone can move at your speed. You need to learn strategies to prepare people for new ideas; you need to take the time to bring people with you; you need to learn when to give others the information, assurance, and space they need to move forward with confidence.

She was absolutely right. When I was growing up, my family came to dread it when I would say "Hey! I have a great idea!" and fly out the door, expecting them all to keep up. And when I became a music teacher, the day of a concert was still a work in progress – if I saw a better way of doing things, I would just change it up, expecting everyone to run with it despite all the planning and decisions the team had already made. I know that a lot of my challenges at work come when others can't respond as quickly as I want them to.

That was the most helpful professional development I have ever had. I've been working on slowing down, communicating better, and letting go of last-minute initiatives ever since.

This idea of flipping the coin has stayed with me. When I think of teachers that I have coached, observed, and worked with, it rings true.

- A teacher I once coached believed her teaching strength was in her organization and systems, the detailed way she scaffolded student learning step by step, and the carefully prepared lesson plans. This teacher's weaknesses were her inflexibility and lack of response to her students. Her micro-managing disempowered students and dampened their agency.
- A teacher I worked with considered himself strict and in control, was proud that he kept a firm handle on student behavior, and "ran a tight ship." I noticed that this teacher tended to make students feel oppressed, overpowered, and disrespected.
- Another teacher I knew prided herself on "really getting" the students – having great relationships with them, being the one that students chose to be a confidante. Unfortunately, she made some students feel uncomfortable: they perceived this behavior as over-closeness. Some students felt that she "played favorites." The result: loss of respect and credibility in her classroom.

When we build self-awareness, it is important to recognize our strengths. Chances are, your administrators, parents, and students have given you positive feedback about certain aspects of your teaching. Those things you do well, those things about your teaching that have received compliments are worth celebrating, *and* this is the best place to start when you are looking for a Blindspot. The best indicator of the flippable coin is something about your teaching that makes you feel proud.

Pride can be the give-away. The quote at the beginning of this chapter eloquently points this out. Everyone is secretly proud of something about their practice. You create beautiful bulletin boards, you are a stickler when it comes to due dates, you understand your student's social-emotional needs… You *should* be proud! It is perfectly okay to know what you do well. And if there is a little hubris mixed into your pride, all the better, because hubris – that feeling that you do that thing a little better than everyone else – may well mark the spot where your Blindspot treasure is buried.

You may have to sit quietly and meditate on this. Journaling helps. What is one aspect of teaching that you do better than everybody else? If you were the kind of person who could be smug (which I'm sure you're not), what would you be – even just a tiny bit – smug about?

Try this journaling exercise: write down five things about teaching that you know you do well. Now, if you were forced to brag about one of them, which would it be? What is the one thing that you do better than everyone else at your school? (Or everyone else in your circle of colleagues.) You can be honest, because you won't be showing this to anyone.

Now, take that thing and flip it around. That, potentially, is your Blindspot.

Here are some examples of "flipped coins":

Area of strength – you are:	*Other side of the coin – you **may** be:*
Great at delivering lectures – you teach through fabulous PowerPoint slides, or you are a good orator.	Allowing your voice to dominate in the classroom, failing to listen to or to foster student voice (Blindspot #1)
Super-prepared – with lesson plans, unit plans, etc.	Unable to respond to real-time student needs and learning, unable to take advantage of students' interests, questions, curiosity; stuck on the plan; inflexible (Blindspot #4).

(Continued)

(Continued)

Area of strength – you are:	*Other side of the coin – you **may** be:*
Super-organized – with classroom systems, classroom management, and efficient routines.	Unable to see what students really need in the moment; too focused on rules and regulations to foster strong relationships (Blindspot #3).
Relatable, friendly, well-liked by students – a trusted confidante.	Not enough professional distance, "playing favorites," inconsistent treatment of students, uncomfortably close (Blindspot #7).
Responsive to students' needs – flexible and adaptable.	Disorganized, students not having enough structure or clarity to feel secure (Blindspot #5).
Clear – good at creating step-by-step learning sequences.	Steps for success are too small, depriving students of their ability to think and inquire (Blindspot #3, Blindspot #4).
A big-ideas person – teaching large concepts and over-arching themes rather than details.	Not enough rigor; students unable to grasp the details needed to fully engage in the learning (Blindspot # 8).
Tough, "hard-ass," giving kids the boundaries they need.	Students perceive you as cold, harsh, mean (Blindspot #10).

I need to emphasize this: the other side of the coin is your *potential* Blindspot. Not every teacher who is responsive to student needs is disorganized. Just because you create clear systems and are good at classroom management doesn't mean you are necessarily cold, harsh, and mean. Not at all. Just that this might be a place to *consider*, as you search for your Blindspot.

This idea of the flipped coin goes back to the work of Carl Jung, the father of analytical psychology. Jung developed the concept of "the shadow": the unconscious aspect of the personality that does not correspond with the ego ideal (Perry, 2015). The shadow is the self's emotional Blindspot. Coaches and therapists sometimes use this shadow metaphor to uncover a hidden side of the persona. Gourov and Lomas (2019) call the shadow "a goldmine for personal growth" (p. 1). By bringing irrational and limiting behaviors to light, coaches who use this technique find that their clients become unstuck and are able to move on with their lives (du Toit, 2016). Coaching with the shadow in mind is similar to this idea of flipping the coin.

When we examine our strengths – in particular, those aspects of our work about which we feel a certain amount of pride – and then peer into the underside, we may see opportunities we were missing before: opportunities for growth. And that is what it's all about, isn't it?

As for me? I still think I'm pretty darn good at being responsive to students' needs – following their lead and improvising learning moments that reflect students' thinking, interests, and receptivity. I love how well I can come up with great ideas and implement them on the spot. So… I'm working hard at being better organized (Blindspot #6): I am trying to focus my energy on providing students with clarity around expectations, assessment, and evaluation, and I am trying to do better with communicating with colleagues ahead of time about my ideas. It's an uphill battle, but I am noticing improvement. Thank you, Lois!

References

Du Toit, D. H. (2016). An archetypal approach to coaching. In L. E. van Zyl, M. W. Stander, & A. Odendaal (Eds.), *Coaching psychology: Meta-theoretical perspectives and applications in multicultural contexts* (pp. 187–203). Springer International Publishing.

Gourov, D., & Lomas, T. (2019). 'It's about wholeness. I love my awesomeness and I love my flawesomeness': An IPA analysis of coaching with the shadow in mind. *The Coaching Psychologist, 15*(2), 11–21.

Perry, C. (2015, August 12). *The Jungian shadow – Society of analytical psychology.* The Society of Analytical Psychology. https://www.thesap.org.uk/articles-on-jungian-psychology-2/about-analysis-and-therapy/the-shadow/

5

Sit in Others' Classrooms

> There are these two young fish swimming along and they happen to meet an older fish swimming the other way, who nods at them and says "Morning, boys. How's the water?" And the two young fish swim on for a bit, and then eventually one of them looks over at the other and goes "What the hell is water?"
> — David Foster Wallace (2009)

Have you ever done a workout that was a little different from your usual one? Perhaps you stay fit by running, but then one day you go paddleboarding. The next day, you've got sore muscles you didn't even know you had. The soreness in places you've never been sore before indicates that while you may be super-fit in one area, there are aspects of fitness (i.e., some muscle groups) that you haven't considered.

Sitting in others' classrooms is just like that. Simply by going into a colleague's class and watching them teach, you will notice things that never occurred to you before. You may see a terrific organizational system that keeps track of students' papers. You may notice a technique that the teacher uses to grab the class's attention or an arrangement of classroom furniture that fosters student collaboration. You may see instructional techniques that you have heard of or read about but never actually witnessed

DOI: 10.4324/9781003490975-8

being used successfully. You may see a lesson delivered in a way you would never have considered possible.

You may also notice things that your colleague does that would not work for you. I had a colleague who was hilarious – the jokes and asides kept the students engaged like nothing I'd ever seen before. It worked for him, but that's not me. I'm just not that funny. And that's okay. Sitting in others' classrooms doesn't mean you have to imitate everything that works for that teacher.

In fact, sitting in others' classrooms does require you to sort the wheat from the chaff. You will undoubtedly also see things that don't work well. And you may notice things that clearly sit within that teacher's Blindspot – for example, a tendency to repeat the same instructions again and again (Blindspot #1) or valuable class time wasted by a painfully slow attendance-taking process (Blindspot #4). Seeing these Blindspots in real time and reflecting on what isn't working are just as valuable as observing excellent teaching. Truly, for me, sitting in others' classrooms and witnessing good – and not so good – teaching have been, by far, the primary ways that I've developed my practice.

Remember, this strategy of "sitting in others' classrooms" is not about giving feedback. We'll get to that in Chapter 6, and that is a whole other kettle of fish. This is simply about you getting yourself into other classrooms to broaden your concept of what teaching looks like, in as many varied forms and formats as possible.

The fact of the matter is that teachers tend to practice in isolation. Studies show how rare it is for teachers to watch their colleagues teach (e.g., Darling-Hammond & Ball, 1998). Judith Warren Little and Lieberman (1987) described the situation 25 years ago, still apt today:

> In large numbers of schools, and for long periods of time, teachers are colleagues in name only. They work out of sight and hearing of one another, plan and prepare their lessons and materials alone, and struggle on their own to solve most of their instructional, curricular and management problems.
>
> (p. 165)

And yet, in their research paper *How the Best Performing School Systems Come Out on Top*, Barber and Mourshed (2007) found that in high-performing schools, teachers regularly invite each other into each other's classrooms to observe. Note that this research says nothing about providing or receiving feedback: the marker of high-performing schools was simply the cross-pollination that results from teachers sitting in each other's classrooms.

Hendry and Oliver (2012) found that watching a colleague teach is more beneficial than receiving feedback. Similarly, Bell and Mladenovic (2008) interviewed 32 tutors who had paired up, observed each other teach, discussed with their partner what they had observed, then provided feedback to each other. Most of the interviewees spoke about the benefits gained from simply watching their partner teach. Only two of the 32 said that the feedback given by their colleague was valuable.

In my work as an instructional coach, getting teachers into each other's classrooms to observe has easily been the most effective way to shift teachers' thinking about what is possible. One teacher who relied on his loud voice, presence, and lectures to deliver instruction (Blindspot #1) was frankly amazed when he observed a colleague's discussion-based class. He had no idea that students could be so responsive when provided with appropriate scaffolds. Another teacher who struggled with classroom management made tremendous improvement after observing the effectiveness and efficiency of another teacher's classroom routines. In my own case, I learned how to use every teaching minute effectively by watching Tony Araujo run choir rehearsals. His classes have more than 100 students in them, yet he engages all the students all the time, using strategies I never would have known about had I not sat in his classes. You can't see what you can't see until you change your perspective.

How does sitting in others' classes help us find our Blindspot? It gets us out of our personal fishbowl, where, like the youngsters in David Foster Wallace's story (quoted at the beginning of this chapter), we may lack awareness. Sitting in others' classrooms gives us a broader vantage point from which to observe our own practice. Just like travelling to a foreign country gives you perspective about your own culture, simply spending time in classrooms other than your own, observing, noticing, and thinking, can give you your aha! moment.

The research. An interesting study that took place in secondary schools was conducted by Burgess, Rawal, and Taylor in 2021. These researchers randomly chose 82 secondary schools in England and, within those schools, randomly assigned year 10 and 11 math and English teachers to observe, or be observed by, a peer. Observers used a rubric based on Charlotte Danielson's Framework for Teaching (2007) to evaluate observees' performance after six to 12 observations. The results showed that students in classes whose teachers were involved in the Peer Observation treatment performed better on final exams than controls. Clearly, both watching and being watched had positive effects on those teachers' students' test scores. What I find fascinating is that the students whose teachers were ***observers*** fared slightly better than students whose teachers ***were observed***. Simply going into another's class to watch someone else teach – and thinking about that person's teaching – was more beneficial than being watched and receiving feedback.

In fact, throwing feedback into the mix can effectively halt the entire proposition. Studies found that teachers were reluctant to partake in peer observations when feedback was expected (Dos Santos, 2016). They feared scrutiny, whether or not evaluations were for formative or summative purposes (Adshead et al., 2006).

I would too. The prospect of receiving feedback from a peer is fraught with difficulties. The next chapter of this book provides a way forward for receiving feedback from peers. For now, though, Sitting in Others' Classrooms is simply about observing: sitting and seeing what there is to see in others' classrooms – and using this as grist for the mill as you search for your Blindspot.

So. Easy to say, hard to do, given the day-to-day reality of a teacher's life. It's not like you can just take your next prep block and randomly turn up in someone else's classroom. Especially if you work in a school where peer observation is ***not*** the norm, where teachers work behind closed doors and are very private about what happens in their classrooms. Best to begin with small steps.

1. Approach a colleague who seems relatively open and tell them you have heard positive things (possibly from students) about a particular aspect of their teaching.
2. Ask if you could come in to observe that particular, specific thing (the way they begin their class, for example). Chances are they will be flattered and welcoming and will schedule a time for you to come and observe. (Say thank you.)
3. When you observe the class, notice other aspects of their teaching (their questioning techniques, their classroom layout, their use of wait time, for example). Be complimentary about those additional things and ask if you can have a follow-up, longer visit to observe those other specific things.
4. Have a conversation about what you learned from observing and let them know how beneficial it was for you to watch them teach.
5. Mention that you would love the school to become more "open-door" because it has been so helpful to your practice. This teacher may mention the exchange to their colleagues, and the idea may begin to circulate in staffroom conversations. This will plant the seed for future peer observation opportunities.

Here are other actions you can take to help create a school climate of "open doors":

- Encourage others to visit ***your*** classroom. If conditions require that your door stay literally closed while you teach (e.g., to keep out sound from the hallway), you could consider putting a sign on your door with something like: "Please come in! We love having visitors in our classroom!" A sign like this can be removed at times when you need privacy: when students are writing a test or when your class is discussing a sensitive topic.
- An extension to this idea: you could add to your sign a "Please notice …" and write something that you are being intentional about in your practice. I like to write

"Please notice that students are learning to work collaboratively" when I am intentionally allowing students to work on group-work projects with minimal teacher support. Without such a sign, an observer might only notice that the class seems a bit chaotic (for now), that the product may not be up to standard (yet), and that I appear to be disengaged from the students' struggles. The sign makes my intentions and goals as an educator evident.

- You may find that others follow your lead, thus paving the way to a school-wide norm of open doors.

If you already have a teaching partner with whom you regularly co-teach, or if you already work closely with one or two other teachers, you may still need to broaden your reach. I worked with a set of four teachers within a department who were constantly in each other's classes. They continually provided each other with mutual support and were a trusted sounding board for each other's practice. However, they all taught with a similar style – and they shared the same Blindspot. Until they observed teachers outside of their tightly-knit group, they struggled to conceptualize alternative pedagogical possibilities.

If you are a singleton teacher – the only kindergarten teacher in the school or the only second language teacher, for example – you will still benefit from watching teachers teach other subjects and age groups. However, nothing beats watching someone else teach your specialty area. Use your contacts, your district's professional groups, and your principal's contacts to get yourself into a class in another school. A reasonable administrator may well support this initiative by giving you release time.

Having said this, teaching schedules can make it tricky to get yourself into others' classrooms in real time. The next-best alternative is to watch teacher videos. Footage is available through various teaching improvement websites, where specific teaching concepts are illustrated with live clips of teaching practice. By watching such videos, you will get a sense not only of the concept the video is meant to demonstrate but also of other aspects of teaching you may not have encountered before.

- The *Teach Like A Champion* website (https://teachlikeachampion.org/) has lots of classroom footage with detailed comments about what is working in these classrooms.
- The *Teaching Channel* website (https://learn.teachingchannel.com/videos) has hundreds of videos of teachers teaching to illustrate various techniques (there is a cost to subscribe).

However, these are small snapshots and won't give you the holistic experience of observing in real-time, in three dimensions, in a real classroom.

I profoundly believe that the best use of professional development funds is to provide teachers with release time so that they can sit in others' classrooms. Show your principal this chapter. Show them the research. Invite their cooperation to make it happen more often.

References

Adshead, L., White, P. T., & Stephenson, A. (2006). Introducing peer observation of teaching to GP teachers: A questionnaire study. *Medical teacher*, *28*(2), e68–e73.

Barber, M., & Mourshed, M. (2007). *How the world's best-performing school systems come out on top*. McKinsey & Company.

Bell, A., & Mladenovic, R. (2008). The benefits of peer observation of teaching for tutor development. *Higher Education*, *55*(6), 735–752.

Burgess, S., Rawal, S., & Taylor, E. S. (2021). Teacher peer observation and student test scores: Evidence from a field experiment in English secondary schools. *Journal of Labor Economics*, *39*(4), 1155–1186.

Danielson, C. (2007). *Enhancing professional practice: A framework for teaching*. Association for Supervision and Curriculum Development.

Darling-Hammond, L., & Ball, D. L. (1998). Teaching for high standards: What policymakers need to know and be able to do. National Commission on Teaching and America's Future and Consortium for Policy Research in Education.

Dos Santos, L. M. (2016). Foreign language teachers' professional development through peer observation programme. *English Language Teaching*, *9*(10), 39–46.

Hendry, G.D., & Oliver, G.R. (2012). Seeing is believing: The benefits of peer observation. *Journal of University Teaching & Learning Practice*, *9*(1). http://ro.uow.edu.au/jutlp/vol9/iss1/7

Little, J. W., & Lieberman, A. (1987). Teachers as colleagues. In A. Lieberman (Ed.), *Schools as Collaborative Cultures: Creating the Future Now* (pp. 165–193). Falmer Press.

Wallace, D.F. (2009). *This is water: Some thoughts, delivered on a significant occasion, about living a compassionate life*. Little, Brown.

6

Forced Choice

> What matters is how things are taught, rather than what is taught. — Dylan Wiliam (2011)

Teaching is personal. When you are a teacher, it is your life, your purpose, your calling. We identify strongly with our teaching. Our sense of self is tied up with how well we believe we teach.

What we teach – our subject, the curriculum, our assessment methods, etc. – is external. It is typically dictated by regulators or administrators. Being told to shift our focus from content to competencies (for example) may result in a challenging shift in our practice, but it doesn't feel as personal, somehow, as ***how*** we teach. And as Wiliam says (above), the ***how*** matters more.

How we teach is very personal. How we manage ourselves and our students, how we create a classroom experience for students, how we relate to students and nurture their relationships with us – this speaks to who we are as people. As such, the ego gets seriously involved. Tell me we're shifting our school's curricular focus, so now my courses need to incorporate project-based learning? Sure, I can learn how to do that. But tell me I use a baby voice when I talk to my students (Blindspot #2)? Ouch!

Most feedback that addresses ***how*** we teach creates an inference about how "good" we are as a teacher. This is why having others observe our teaching can be a terrifying experience. We feel

DOI: 10.4324/9781003490975-9

on display. We feel judged. This is the reason most teachers like to teach behind closed doors. This is why most teachers prefer to have their own classroom rather than share a class: they want to be able to work out the bugs in their practice without feeling evaluated by another teacher present in the room. And this is the reason we don't love the administrator "pop in" and we dread our administrator's annual formal observation. Want to look at my curriculum planning documents? No problem! But you want to come into my classroom and watch me teach? No way.

Receiving feedback is even worse than being observed. A "suggestion" inevitably feels like a criticism. A criticism turns into the thought that we are teaching badly – and now we have a wounded sense of self. The painful feelings that emanate from this wounding are the essence of shame.

Brené Brown, a leader in research on shame and vulnerability, called shame "the intensely painful feeling or experience of believing that we are flawed and therefore unworthy of love, belonging, and connection" (Brown, 2018, p. 126). Brown explained that experiencing feelings of shame is universal: everyone (except sociopaths) experiences shame, but no one talks about it. Proof: when was the last time a colleague admitted to you that they were ashamed of some aspect of their teaching? When was the last time you spoke up in a staff meeting, or in the staffroom, about the fact that you were embarrassed by your teaching shortcomings?

Shame compels us to gird our loins for that annual evaluation meeting because we fear that our weaknesses will be pointed out. Shame makes us believe that any feedback we receive (other than positives) means that we are less-than, we are not good enough, and we are flawed. No matter how hard we try to remember that teaching evaluations are meant to focus on our strengths and lead to professional growth, feelings of shame tend to dwarf positive expectations.

In the end, though, in any teacher evaluation context, you aren't likely to hear feedback related to any of the Classic Ten Blindspots. Why? Because each of the Classic Ten is ***personal***. They are the tough-love, hard-to-hear, potentially harsh-landing truth-bombs. Which is why we rarely hear about them in feedback sessions. Who has the guts to deliver this kind of message?

I have noticed that administrators, instructional coaches, and colleagues – myself included – have a propensity to chicken out when it comes to giving teachers critical feedback related to the Classic Ten. We go for the easy stuff: lots of positives and then perhaps a slight suggestion of a superficial tweak the teacher could easily make. Research confirms this to be true: Eliezer Yariv (2006) found that elementary school principals in his study were reluctant to submit negative feedback to teachers. Instead, they frequently chose to say nothing rather than provide constructive criticism (he called this the "mum effect"). Wragg et al. (2000) also found that secondary school principals tended to choose maintaining good relations with teachers over keeping high standards. Bridges (2013) described school principals who

> ignored or overlooked the poor performance, filled written observation reports sprinkled with glowing generalities such as "I really enjoyed my visit." They used double-talk in written evaluations to muffle criticism of the teacher performance, and inflated performance ratings in the mistaken belief that these evaluations would act as positive reinforcement.
>
> (p. 148)

It seems that few administrators are up to the job of delivering hard, much-needed feedback. And it's not likely you have a colleague willing to do it either. A highly skilled instructional coach *might* lead you to self-discover your Blindspot, eventually. But who is lucky enough to have a highly skilled instructional coach? In 25 years of teaching, I never had one.

This is where the "Forced Choice" method (below) comes in. It is a way to get the feedback you need – honest, useful feedback about your teaching. Although it does require you to involve a trusted colleague and will involve that colleague watching you teach, the rules are designed to remove the shame and vulnerability from the equation and to protect your colleague from risk of retribution. So grab a partner, take a deep breath, and use Forced Choice to find your Blindspot.

How to Implement Forced Choice

- Choose a colleague whom you trust. This must be someone in a non-evaluative position. You need to trust that this strategy will be used purely for teacher improvement and not feed in any way into the teacher evaluation process.
- Give this colleague opportunities to know your teaching. Perhaps they are already familiar with your work (you share a teaching space, for example). Or it may be someone that you will invite into your classroom for a series of observations. A one-off observation won't do: you need your person to have enough information to be able to identify ***patterns*** of teaching behavior.
- Provide this colleague with the list of Ten Classic Blindspots. (Appendix C lists the Blindspots with a concise explanation of each one.)
- Tell your colleague that they are to identify one of the Ten that is your primary Blindspot. They must identify the one – and only one – that, if addressed, would most improve your practice.
- They are **not** allowed to say "none of them" – as this would imply that you have no faults and are a "perfect teacher" – in other words, giving this option transforms the exercise into an evaluation.
- Nor are they permitted to say "all of them." This would imply that you have many faults and are therefore a "bad teacher."
- Neither may they identify several Blindspots or even two. It could be that you talk too much (Blindspot #1) and also have vocal hazards that need fixing (#3). However, your colleague must prioritize, and they must pick (and mention) one and only one.
- They may not quantify the extent of your Blindspot. They may not say "Well, I suppose if I had to pick one, then maybe number 3 – but only a little." Nor may they say "Wow, you've got serious #7." They only get to indicate which one, not how much.

These constraints remove judgment from the picture. They keep this exercise out of the evaluative space. It's not you, it's the rules – it is the exercise's fault that your colleague must pick one Blindspot. (Blame it on me if you want to.)

Because the rules are clear, your feelings cannot be hurt. Regardless of which Blindspot your trusted colleague points to, there is no evaluation here. You forced them to choose one. All they are doing is indicating that, if they ***had*** to pick one (and they do), this would be the one for you to prioritize.

It may surprise you to find out which Blindspot your colleague chooses. You may feel that they chose incorrectly. You may wish to repeat this exercise with another colleague, to get a second opinion. Or try it out with a few colleagues. By the time you have three colleagues all telling you that your biggest issue is that students in your class are afraid to make mistakes (Blindspot #9), it should be clear to you that this is indeed valid feedback. And then you are in a position to do something about it. (See Part III of this book.)

You may wish to combine "Forced Choice" with other strategies from this section of the book to triangulate your evidence. Once the evidence starts to converge on a single Blindspot, you will have a clear indication of where to dig for your professional development gold.

If You Are a Teacher Invited to Deliver Forced Choice

If you are asked by a colleague to do a Forced Choice for them, the task is straightforward. Get familiar with the list of Ten Classic Blindspots (see Appendix C). Schedule some observations if you aren't already familiar with their teaching. Reflect on your colleague's teaching. Consider which one of the Blindspots, if addressed, would have the most significant impact on student learning.

What should you do if you detect multiple Blindspots in your colleague's practice? Prioritize. **Choose only one**. No one can address multiple Blindspots at the same time: teachers need to focus their energy on one thing. Next year, after your colleague has successfully addressed one Blindspot, they can repeat the process – maybe with you, maybe with someone else – and the next critical Blindspot can be addressed.

Remember: **this is not a teacher evaluation**. This is about teacher development. I once coached a teacher who had all but one of the Blindspots. All but one. Yes, if we were evaluating performance for the purpose of re-hiring or for compensation decisions, then all aspects of her teaching would need consideration. But this was not the objective then, and it is not the objective now. **The goal is simply to improve teaching**. And no one can improve everything at once. So pick one. Just one.

In some cases, addressing one Blindspot can have a spillover effect. For example, if a teacher is wasting time in class (Blindspot #6), addressing this may well improve their organizational skills (Blindspot #5), because in order to use every minute effectively, they will have to invest time in planning. Similarly, a teacher who talks too much (Blindspot #1) may, in attending to their speaking tendencies, become aware of their verbal hazards (Blindspot #2) and fix them. So it is possible to hit two pins with one ball by revealing only one Blindspot.

Another tricky situation would be the teacher who has no Blindspots. Not a single one. They are perfect, in every way. What if they have asked you to identify their Blindspot? What then?

Sorry to burst your bubble. This teacher doesn't exist. *Everyone*'s practice can benefit from improvement to any one of the Classic Ten. The question will ***always*** be ***which one***.

What if you observe something that is not on the list? Should you tell them that they have Blindspot #11? And that this particular area is more important to their practice than any of the ten on the list?

My answer to that is: **no**. Play by the rules. If you go beyond the Classic Ten, you are making a de facto evaluation. The point of Forced Choice is that it takes away from you the responsibility that comes with pointing out a flaw. Forced Choice allows you to essentially say: "You are fabulous. Really top-notch. So many great things going on in your classroom. But since I ***have*** to pick one …"

Furthermore, if you are given the freedom to go outside the Ten, you might let yourself – and your partner – off the hook by choosing something easy and impersonal. Something superficial, like: their bulletin boards could use nicer borders. Best to stick to the Classic Ten – this way, you can blame the rules of the game, provide useful feedback, and keep your and your colleague's self-esteem intact.

You cannot see your own face: you need a mirror to reflect it back to yourself. And not one of those judgey mirrors – no one needs to hear that they are, or are not, the fairest one in the land. You just need to see if you have lettuce in your teeth.

Similarly, to raise your self-awareness as a teacher, you need clear, non-judgmental feedback. You don't need a score on a rubric or an evaluative phrase (such as "limited, emerging, developing, proficient"). You just need to know what that one thing is that will have the most impact on your teaching. The one thing that you can't see, so that you can get working on addressing it.

So grab a colleague, sit them down, and make them choose from the list of the Classic Ten. Then say "thank you," buy them a coffee, and fix that one thing.

References

Bridges, E. M. (2013). *The incompetent teacher: Managerial responses* (Vol. 15). Routledge.

Brown, B. (2018). *Dare to lead: Brave work. Tough conversations. Whole hearts*. Random House.

Wiliam, D. (2011). *Embedded formative assessment*. Solution Tree Press.

Wragg, E.C., Haynes, G.S., Wragg, C.M. & Chamberlin, R.P. (2000) *Failing teachers?* Routledge.

Yariv, E. (2006). Mum effect: Principals' reluctance to submit negative feedback. *Journal of Managerial Psychology*, *21*(6), 533–546. https://doi.org/10.1108/02683940610684382

7

Student Input

Calvin:	"Here's the latest poll on your performance as dad. Your approval rating is pretty low, I'm afraid."
Dad:	"That's because there's not necessarily any connection between what's good and what's popular. I do what's right, not what gets approval."
Calvin:	"You'll never keep the job with that attitude."
Dad:	"If someone else offers to do it, let me know." — Bill Watterson (1989)

Our students observe us day in, day out, and as we know, are very perceptive. Since the entire reason for improving our teaching is to improve our students' learning and experience in our class, it makes sense to listen to their voices. They know better than anyone how we can serve them better.

Or do they? As the quote from *Calvin and Hobbes* illustrates, what students say they want may not be best for them. Believe me, if I had a nickel for every time my students filled out an end-of-year survey with requests to watch more movies in class…

The research is mixed on this question. At the university level, where end-of-term questionnaires are the norm, there is a plethora of research on the value of student ratings of their professors. The results are mixed. Kornell and Hausman (2016),

DOI: 10.4324/9781003490975-10

having reviewed thousands of studies on whether better teachers get better ratings, were unable to draw any general conclusions because the results were so varied. However, they highlighted one important finding – that teachers who make larger contributions to **long-term** student learning, as measured by performance in subsequent courses – received ***lower*** teacher ratings than teachers whose students did better on end-of-term exams (see especially Carrell & West, 2010; Braga et al., 2014). Kornell and Hausman concluded that "students do not necessarily have the expertise to recognize good teaching… In the end, student ratings bear more than a passing similarity to a popularity contest" (p. 7). And these are university students! How can we expect high school, or elementary school, students to do any better?

Well, a lot comes down to the feedback "instrument" used – the particular survey, questionnaire, or feedback form. A rigorous, well-regarded study by Wilkerson (2000) compared student, principal, and self-ratings to tests of students' performance in reading, language arts, and mathematics. The project involved 988 students from K-12, 35 teachers, and four principals in a Wyoming school district – so lots of data, lots of rigor. The main finding was that the student ratings of teachers **were indeed** the best predictor of student achievement, compared with principals' ratings and teachers' self-evaluations. The principals' teacher evaluations didn't even come close. The researchers concluded that students – even kindergarteners – ***can*** discriminate teacher performance in relation to their own learning. And they can do it better than the adults.

When I read Wilkerson (2000), I had to ask: what were the survey instruments that the students used? And what were the tests that measured the students' learning? If better teaching means preparing kids better for content-heavy testing, then maybe the students weren't the experts Wilkerson made them out to be.

First, the student questionnaires. The researchers chose to use questions that focused on specific teacher behaviors, rather than teacher evaluation, in order to avoid a "leniency bias" (the tendency of an evaluator to mark a rating scale toward the high end). They were concerned that leniency bias might creep into younger students' feedback, given young students' tendency to become emotionally attached to their teachers. So the questions focused on easily identifiable teacher behaviors. For example:

- My teacher explains the rules for classroom behavior very clearly.
- My teacher likes it when we ask questions.
- My teacher is easy to understand when talking.
- My teacher makes our work interesting.

(Questions were sourced from Omotani, 1992)

Students gave their responses on a five-point Likert scale (1 = never; 5 = almost always).

Students' learning was measured by criterion-referenced tests developed by the school district, designed to correlate with the Stanford Eighth Edition Achievement Tests in reading, language arts, and mathematics*. Okay, if doing well on the Stanford Achievement Tests is the goal, then it seems that the teacher behaviors listed on the questionnaire, do the trick.

This research is over 30 years old – but I find it compelling because it seems to have cracked the code for eliciting helpful student feedback: surveying for teacher behaviors. And nothing published since has so rigorously examined the relationship between K-12 students' ratings and achievement results.

In a more recent study, one limited to middle and high school, Balch (2012) compared student survey results and student achievement in Georgia. The study used survey results from 12,408 students, randomly sampled from 95 middle and high schools. Balch's research used the Tripod (Ferguson, 2010)

* For teachers who don't work in the United States, the Stanford Achievement Test Series is a set of standardized, norm-referenced achievement tests used by school districts in the U.S., taken by millions of children from kindergarten through to high school each year. It is now in its 10th version and often referred to as the "Stanford 10" or SAT-10. (not to be confused with the SAT college admission test published by the College Board).

student surveys. Similar to those used in the Wilkerson study, these surveys used a Likert scale (1 = rarely, 5 = always), and questions were tied to observable teacher behaviors. For example:

- My teacher seems to know if something is bothering me.
- The teacher consistently provides assistance as needed.
- My teacher is a very good listener when kids talk to her/him.
- My teacher makes lessons interesting.

(Ferguson, 2010)

The results: Balch found links (positive but only marginally significant) between the student survey results and student achievement gains in middle and high school English Language Arts, science, and social studies. However, while high school math also showed a positive relationship between achievement and survey results, middle school math showed none.

Do students notice improvements after giving their teachers feedback? Sometimes. A meta-analysis of 19 studies that measured changes in students' perceptions of teaching found a small but significant positive effect (Röhl, 2021). This means that the students noticed teacher improvement after they had given feedback – some of the time.

Again, the usefulness of teacher surveys is always going to come back to the questions that are asked on the survey. My concern with the student feedback tools used in the research cited above is that they focus on particular ways to teach: they provide a fairly exhaustive list of teacher behaviors that are (according to the research) somewhat correlated with student success. Are we confusing correlation with causation here? Do these survey questions really get at the thing that teachers need to address, the things that will make a big impact on student learning?

You can have students go through a lengthy list of teacher behaviors, evaluating each one, but if you don't list the right behaviors, you'll never know (for example) if you are micromanaging (Blindspot #3) or have a vocal hazard (Blindspot #2).

John Hattie pointed out that "We know, for example, if a student believes that the teacher has no credibility, then the teacher is unlikely to have much impact—even if they are using all the desirable teacher strategies with great classroom climates" (Hattie, 2012, p. viii).

Furthermore, asking students to rate things like "my teacher makes lessons interesting" sounds a bit vague to me and seems to invite a leniency bias. In order to send a strong message, an item would need to turn up really low scores. Are kids capable of putting their empathy aside? I know from conversations with students that they really worry about hurting their teachers' feelings – even the ones they don't like.

My sense is that as long as we are asking kids to evaluate their teachers – for example, rating items on a scale of 1 to 5 – a whole lot of feelings get mixed up in the process. The way students feel about their teacher, their emotional connection, and the knowledge that their teacher will see the results all come into play. So can retribution: if a student feels reactive about low grades they have recently received, or has been recently reprimanded, this could lower the ratings they give (called the "horns effect"). The solution is to take evaluation off the table when we ask students for feedback.

What about open-ended questions? If students are invited to give written feedback rather than an evaluative score, would this be useful? Alhija and Fresko (2009) studied this very question – with university students. They found that most of the student comments they collected were too general to be useful. However, they did note that some written comments related to unique aspects of the students' experiences. The researchers concluded that written comments were indeed useful in that they potentially address a broader range of variables than could the survey (closed-ended) questions. I found no research that looked at this question at the K-12 level.

Alhija and Fresko (2009) wrapped up their paper with a useful piece of advice: they recommended that teachers give student surveys at different times throughout the year rather than at the end. This way, teachers can demonstrate their responsiveness.

Students who see that their instructors are attentive to their feedback may be more motivated to write meaningful comments in the future. Good point.

But what open-ended questions are going to get the most useful feedback? There is very little research on this topic at the K-12 level. For me, I always include open-ended questions in my surveys. What have I got to lose? (See Chapter 3 – "Develop a Feedback Mindset".) Here are some examples of questions that have yielded helpful comments for me:

- What kinds of things has Dr. B. done that have helped you to learn better? You can elaborate on specific examples.
- What do you wish Dr. B. had done differently?
- Anything else on your mind?

Can you spot the potential pitfall with the first question? What does "learn better" mean, and what do students think it means? One student may interpret "learn better" as being able to score higher on the test; another may interpret "learn better" as making the learning as fun as possible (i.e., more movies); while a third (albeit mythical) student could conceptualize "learn better" as being provided with rich and varied opportunities to grow as a fully self-actualized human being. Well, despite this murkiness, I maintain that open invitations can yield useful information if you're willing to sift through the comments and sort the helpful from the unhelpful.

But will responses to a student questionnaire reveal your Blindspot? Will your students take up this open invitation to zero in on the one thing that you really need to address to improve your teaching? Do they even know what that thing is?

Again, students – especially the younger ones – worry about being mean. The odd one may be willing to drop a truth bomb, but most aren't going to say the thing you need to hear, even in an anonymous written comment. Most kids just can't get their heads around a reversal of the power dynamic. Many students still struggle with the idea that critical feedback can be a good thing.

One solution is to make the survey's purpose clear to students from the outset. Be explicit that this questionnaire is not about evaluating your practice but purely about giving helpful feedback. Don't use the words "Assessment" or "Evaluation" in the title of the form. Call it something like "End-of-Term Teacher Feedback." Then, right at the top of the form, provide a written explanation, for example:

> I would like your help to improve my teaching. This is not about whether I am a good teacher – it is about me doing a better job going forward.

Include a note to ensure student safety:

> This form is strictly anonymous. Report cards are done, nothing you say here can impact your grades… and everything you say here will help me become a better teacher going forward! Thank you for your help.

This can help set the stage, putting your students in the right frame of mind to give you feedback.

Next, **do not** use a Likert scale or any other system with numbers or scales that could suggest evaluation. As soon as you ask students to rate things on a scale of 1 to 5, they are going to see this as a way to give their teacher a "grade," which puts them back on the evaluation train. Instead, use Forced Choice (see Chapter 6) as a component of your student feedback process.

The Forced Choice method requires students to choose one from the list of Classic Ten Blindspots that they feel would most improve your teaching and their learning. There will be nothing "mean" or evaluative about their choice – the Classic Ten are equally valid weaknesses. All your students need to do is pick one.

So, on your student survey, in addition to open-ended items soliciting general comments, include something like the following on your questionnaire:

*Choose one of the following areas that Dr. B. should focus on next year. If many apply, pick **the one** that you think would make the most difference to her teaching. If none applies, then still pick one that would improve your class experience in even the slightest way. You can elaborate on your choice below if you like.*

- *Talk less, let students talk more.*
- *Stop micro-managing: students are more capable than she thinks.*
- *Fix the way she talks (examples of the kinds of things that can trip teachers up: uses certain words or phrases too often, speaks in a monotone, speaks in a baby voice, uses upspeak, or speaks too quickly).*
- *Be more responsive to what students need in the moment (rather than always sticking to the plan).*
- *Be more like an adult, less like a BFF.*
- *Be more organized, so that students are clear about what is expected of them.*
- *Use class time more effectively (too many class minutes wasted).*
- *Class is too challenging.*
- *Class is too easy.*
- *Make it safer to make errors (i.e., I'm afraid of making mistakes in Dr. B's class).*
- *I feel that Dr. B. doesn't like me… or I feel that Dr. B. likes some students more than others, which impacts our class.*

Despite the explanation embedded in the instructions, you will find that students still have questions. Answer them!

a) They will ask what to do if none of the items applies. Tell them to pick ***the one*** that applies even marginally – and they can elaborate in the open-ended section. Explain to them that if most students pick that same one – even if it only applies marginally – then that will nevertheless be useful information.
b) Students will wonder what to do if more than one applies. You tell them: prioritize. Which is ***the one*** that will most help improve teaching and learning in your classroom going forward?
c) Students will ask what to do if something else is more of a priority. Ask them to please still pick one and then explain what the something else is in the open-ended section.

The open-ended items (especially "anything else on your mind?"), together with the Forced Choice question, combine a constrained, focused approach with an open, loose approach. This combination, I have found, yields the most revealing information of all.

Interpreting the feedback. Okay. So now you're looking at a stack of papers (or flipping through Google Forms results) with student-written comments and a selection of Blindspot choices. Stop.

Do not look at the results when your students are present. Don't even look at them at school. First, go home, have a snack, pour a cup of tea, and put on your comfy slippers. Sit in a comfortable chair. Take a deep breath. Remind yourself that growth requires courage.

Let's start with the written comments. If you're like me, you will feel heightened emotions as you do your initial scan through the written comments. You will be trying to get a sense of what students are saying, hunting for bits of negativity, while hoping for glowing reviews.

Villa's (2017) research would suggest that this emotional response is entirely normal: Villa found that many teachers experience happiness and curiosity during the feedback and reflection process when the feedback was positive but that some teachers reported anger, sadness, or helplessness when feedback was perceived as negative. According to John Hattie (2021), we will likely go into this exercise with some forward bias – a very human response which makes us interpret good feedback to be about me and negative feedback to be the "ill-informed whims of youngsters (p. vi)". Emotions and bias are going to get in the way of our using this information to help us. They just are.

Try this: First, read the comments through, then put the responses aside and let some time go by. Go back to the written comments later – much later. A few weeks later. Reread them with a fresh set of eyes – but this time, imagine that you are reading another teacher's survey results. Picture this other teacher in your mind. Imagine them to be someone kind, hard-working, and eager to do a good job. Your job is to help this teacher interpret these comments and to advise them how to improve their teaching. Your job is not to evaluate their work but simply to help them level up their practice. Be curious as you go through these comments – see them as a treasure trove offering up clues. What are they telling you about this teacher's best way forward?

Pay close attention to any negative feedback and intentionally check any impulses to dismiss it. After all, this is potentially where you are going to get your best information. At the same time, be kind and compassionate with this teacher and be eager for their growth. What would you say to them? What advice would you offer? Write it down.

Now turn to the Forced Choice question. The nature of Forced Choice is such that it will reveal information only if there are clear patterns. If responses are equally divided amongst a few or more, then chances are that students were not able to pick meaningfully. However, if there is a significant cluster on one Blindspot, this could be telling you something. Compare this with what you found in the written comments.

By looking at this information as if it were about someone else, you can be a little more objective, less reactive, and more curious. It will help to sift out the truly unhelpful (play more movies in class) from the helpful (stop letting disruptive kids waste our time).

Student voice gives us information related to students' conceptions of what it is to be a learner, how they feel about being in your class, and the impact that your teaching has on them. This is powerful information. No, it is not the entire picture. But it is useful for raising self-awareness. Now triangulate your findings with the other strategies listed in this chapter. If you find increasing evidence that Blindspot #2 (for example) should be your priority, then you are ready for Part III of this book.

If you elicit student feedback earlier in the year and then demonstrate to students that you are listening by changing something in response to their comments, then you will not only gain their trust and respect but also be modelling a pro-feedback attitude. That is real power, right there.

Younger students. Filling out written questionnaires is suitable for students from middle school through high school. However, in lower elementary school grades, seeking student voice needs to take a different format. Finding your Blindspot will require you to make inferences from what they tell you about their learning and their classroom. The first step is to engage your students in using their voice to express their experience.

Younger students are able to state preferences. They can tell you what activities they enjoy and what they don't. You can put a large poster on the wall (e.g., with words or pictures of various activities) and tell students to place a checkmark under their most favorite activity and an X under their least favorite activity. You can tally the results and have a class discussion about why they think some things are more popular than others. Then you can ask students to give you suggestions about how to make less popular activities more interesting/engaging/fun.

Ask students: if you were the teacher, what would you do differently? You can do this either as a whole class discussion or as a written project. You can sit with small groups and facilitate this conversation while the rest of the class is at centers.

Engage students in creative storytelling. Begin the story with something like this: "When Sophia grows up, she wants to be a teacher. She wants to be the best teacher in the world. In her classroom, all the kids are happy and they learn a lot. This is what her classroom is like…" Invite students to finish the story from here. They can draw pictures and/or write short narratives to describe Sophia's class.

Interpreting this information will require you to reflect carefully whether any of the input can inform your teaching. No, maybe you can't have a pony in the classroom, but perhaps you can incorporate other ways for students to nurture another living thing (class pet? plants?). For one of my kindergarten students, Sophia's classroom had a tree growing in the middle. They may have seen something like this in a movie. Once the other students heard about this, they all jumped on board, talking about how cool it would be to have a tree in the middle of the class. My compromise? We constructed one out of materials in the school's recycling bin: cardboard boxes, twisted brown paper, lots of tape, paper leaves, and tissue paper blossoms. Not as good as the real thing, but students enjoyed making it, and they felt increased agency because I'd listened, responded to, and facilitated their idea.

What about Blindspots? Will younger students' feedback help you pinpoint which Blindspot you are best able to detect? Possibly. But you will have to read between the lines.

The greatest benefit to listening to Student Input in your classroom is the way it empowers students. Whether or not the feedback points you toward your Blindspot, the fact is, just by asking for it, you show your students that you value their opinion. When you are able to visibly respond to their ideas or requests, you actively demonstrate that they matter. And the very fact that they see you wanting to improve your teaching through feedback models a growth mindset in a very powerful way.

References

Alhija, F. N. A., & Fresko, B. (2009). Student evaluation of instruction: what can be learned from students' written comments? *Studies in Educational Evaluation*, *35*(1), 37–44.

Balch, R. T. (2012). *The validation of a student survey on teacher practice*. Vanderbilt University.

Braga, M., Paccagnella, M., & Pellizzari, M. (2014). Evaluating students' evaluations of professors. *Econ. Educ. Rev.* 41, 71–88. https://doi.org/10.1016/j.econedurev.2014.04.002

Calvin and Hobbes by Bill Watterson for June 12, 1989 | GoComics.com. (1989, June 12). *GoComics*. https://www.gocomics.com/calvinandhobbes/1989/06/12

Carrell, S. E., & West, J. E. (2010). Does professor quality matter? Evidence from random assignment of students to professors. *Journal of Political Economy*, *118*(3), 409–432. https://doi.org/10.1086/653808

Ferguson, R. F. (2010). A guide to tripod's 7Cs framework of effective teaching. https://www.scsk12.org/eps/files/2017/Guide%20to%20Tripod's%207Cs%20Framework.pdf

Hattie, J. (2012). *Visible learning for teachers: Maximizing impact on learning*. Routledge.

Hattie, J. (2021). Forward. In W. Rollett, H. Bijlsma, & W. Röhl (Eds.), *Student feedback on teaching in schools: Using student perceptions for the development of teaching and teachers*. Springer. https://doi.org/10.1007/978-3-030-75150-0

Kornell, N., & Hausman, H. (2016). Do the best teachers get the best ratings? *Frontiers in Psychology*, *7*, 570.

Omotani, L. M. (1992). *Refining valid, reliable and discriminating student feedback items for use as one component of a total teacher performance evaluation system*. Iowa State University.

Röhl, S. (2021). Effects of student feedback on teaching and classes: An overview and meta-analysis of intervention studies. *Student feedback on teaching in schools: Using student perceptions for the development of teaching and teachers*, 139–156.

Villa, L. A. L. (2017). *Teachers taking action with student perception survey data*. Arizona State University.

Wilkerson, D., Manatt, R., Rogers, M., & Maughan, R. (2000). Validation of student, principal, and self-ratings in 360 feedback for teacher evaluation. *Journal of Personnel Evaluation in Education*, *14*(2), 179–192.

8

The Camera Doesn't Lie

> The truth may hurt, but fooling yourself will enslave you. — Charles F. Glassman (2009)

I get it – who's got the time?

Setting up a video recorder (whether it's your phone on a tripod or some other method), filming yourself teaching, and then taking the time to watch the footage – it's a good idea in theory, but when is this ever going to happen?

I have spent years intending to film myself teaching. Never got around to it. When I was working as an instructional coach, I spent an entire school year with a beautiful GoPro camera sitting on my shelf gathering dust. Not only could I not persuade anyone else to use it, but also I couldn't bring myself to film my own teaching block. Too busy. All of us.

However, if I am completely honest with myself, the real reason for my procrastination was the dread of watching myself on camera. Also, the fear of seeing my Blindspot in action kept me from setting up that GoPro. As Glassman said (quoted at the beginning of this chapter), "The truth may hurt."

But if you *were* to video-record yourself teaching – and *if* you were able to forget about it while you were teaching so that it captured your authentic teaching self – and *if* you could bring yourself to watch it, the subsequent viewing would be very

DOI: 10.4324/9781003490975-11

helpful in uncovering your Blindspot. In particular, the following Blindspots, if they exist in your practice, will be glaringly obvious:

- Blindspot #1 – Too much talking. As you watch the video playback, use a timer to record the number of seconds that you are talking, compared to the number of seconds of class time. Now do the math. Research shows that in general, and depending on context, teachers should limit their talking time to 20% to 30% of class time (Kostadinovska-Stojchevska & Popovikj, 2019). More than this would suggest that this might be your Blindspot.
- Blindspot #2 – Vocal hazards. Listen to your voice. Do you hear upspeak? Baby voice? Do you repeat the same phrase or word over and over? It is amazing how we don't notice these things until we see and hear ourselves on video.
- Blindspot #6 – Use every minute. Similar to timing your Teacher Talk (above), as you watch the video playback, use a timer to record the number of minutes that students are being actively engaged in learning, compared to how much time is spent unproductively.
- Blindspot #9 – Making it safe to make mistakes. Notice your tone of voice, choice of words, and facial expression in response to students' attempts, mistakes, and failures. Note also your responses to student success. Pay attention to non-verbals. If you were a student in your class, would you feel pressure to always get the right answer? What would it feel like to make a mistake?

The other Blindspots may not be as evident on video. Use the other strategies in this book to help reveal these – but once you have an inkling, self-video can help to confirm which Blindspot should be your priority.

Video enables teachers to switch their focus from themselves and focus more on the students and their learning. When we are actively instructing the class, we are thinking about what we are saying, the next point, the amount of time left in the class, etc.

We just don't have the bandwidth to focus entirely on the effect we are having on our learners. With video, we can focus in on the students, their reactions, and their body language (provided that the camera is set up to capture the entire class).

What about the research? There is extensive (and I do mean extensive!) research showing that video recordings of teaching and subsequent analysis are valuable tools in teacher development programs:

- to develop reflective practices (McCoy & Lynam, 2021)
- to increase awareness of strengths and weaknesses (Kourieos, 2016)
- to help pre-service teachers identify ways to improve their classroom practice (Hamel & Viau-Guay, 2019).

Hattie's Visible Learning research (Hattie, 2023) reported that video recording, combined with analysis by the teacher and/or other teachers and leaders for the purposes of professional development, results in an effect size of 1.01 – well above the "hinge-point" of 0.4, thus having the potential to considerably accelerate learning. A meta-analysis by Morin et al. (2019) was particularly clear: video analysis is an effective way to improve instruction.

Be Easy on Yourself

The toughest part of using video-recording "selfies" to develop your self-awareness is actually doing it. As I mentioned at the beginning of this section, being self-conscious is the biggest barrier to implementing this technique.

First of all, know that no one needs to see these videos but you. No one is going to use these tapes to evaluate, criticize, or judge your teaching. This practice is just between you and yourself. Sure, instructional coaches, administrators, and teaching support groups can and do use videos to support professional development and teaching evaluation – but what I am recommending here – recording yourself and then watching the playback in order to self-identify your Blindspot – is meant to be safe and private, for your eyes only.

So take it step by step. Make your first goal to just find a place to set up your phone for self-recording. You don't need a tripod or a camera – you just need a phone with enough storage to record about 20 minutes of video. Figure out where you can place the phone so that it will capture a significant part of your teaching. Trickier if you tend to walk around, in which case you would want to film most of the room. And before you film, check with your school's policy on filming in the classroom. Parental consent or notification may be required, even though no one but yourself will see or have access to the video.

Then just do it. Don't wait for a special day or a particular lesson. Just film for the sake of filming. Tell yourself that you don't even have to watch this first one, if that helps you press the record button.

Explain to your students what you are doing. They need to know that you are the only one who will be watching the video and that you will not use it to evaluate their performance. Be clear and upfront about the reason: you want to observe yourself (not them), so that you can improve your teaching. This alone is worth it – to model lifelong learning and commitment to growth and learning.

Once you have filmed yourself, you have broken the initial inertia barrier. Giddyup and film a few more times before you decide to watch the playback, so that you have a few samples to choose from. The more you film yourself, the more you will be used to having the camera rolling. Your behavior will likely become more natural and more representative of the way you teach after you've become accustomed to having a recording device on yourself.

Watching Yourself

As you begin, don't just sit and watch your recordings without an agenda. Instead, put some boundaries in place to keep your overly harsh inner critic at bay:

- First: focus on your behaviors, not your appearance. Leave your hair and wardrobe concerns for another time.
- Imagine that you are watching a colleague or a person you don't know. In your mind, give this teacher a name (not yours), so that you can refer to them in the third person. This may feel a little weird, but it can help overcome the discomfort of watching yourself on video.
- Switch out your judgmental mindset for curiosity. Replace evaluative thoughts ("That was good" or "I sound terrible!") with questions ("I wonder if I needed to say those instructions more slowly?" or "Why did four of the students not understand what to do next?").
- Have the list of Classic Ten Blindspots in front of you. As you watch, go through the list. Consider each Blindspot in turn, focusing on only one at a time. Notice clues that might direct you to any one in particular. You are looking for:
  - #1 – too much teacher talk
  - #2 – verbal hazards: monotone voice, shrill voice, upspeak, baby voice, etc.
  - #3 – micromanaging: too tight control of students' every move
  - #4 – not enough flexibility in response to what students need in the moment
  - #5 – lack of organization
  - #6 – wasted time
  - #7 – teacher behavior that reveals a need to be liked as a peer
  - #8 – signs the lesson or learning activity is too hard or too easy for the students
  - #9 – responses to student errors that might make students afraid to make mistakes
  - #10 – vibes that are mean or angry

Observe your students. Now watch the video again, and this time, observe the students instead of yourself. What are *they* doing? Look for outliers – while many of your students may be actively engaged and eagerly participating, what about the few over there who are not? The one who is sitting quietly and never raises her hand? The two in the corner who are whispering together? How are they experiencing your class? Watching video allows you to focus on the students and see your teaching from their perspective.

When you focus your attention on your students, always follow what I call the Golden Rule of Teaching: **Never blame the kids**. Whatever you see your students doing on the video, take full responsibility. For example, if they are off-task, ask yourself: was my choice of learning activity, text, or materials a bad fit? Did the way I set up the activity, set the expectations, or delivered the instructions contribute to the off-task behavior? What kind of interactions am I having, or not having, with my students that would lead them to make these choices? Remember that what works for one group of students may not work for another: your job is to adjust for the group in front of you.

Sure you can find excuses elsewhere – the students' home life, the previous teacher, too many video games – but in your class, you have tremendous influence. You give that influence away the moment you put the blame elsewhere. In your class, the buck stops with you. As soon as you take full responsibility, you give yourself power to change and grow. So use the magic of modern technology (aka video) to focus your full attention on your students while you are teaching. Their behavior will tell you everything you need to know.

Triangulate. "Triangulation of evidence" is a term used by researchers to mean using multiple datasets, methods, and theories to address a research question. Your research question is: "What am I not aware of that I need to address in order to improve my teaching?" In other words, "What is my Blindspot?" In the language of research, using multiple methods to uncover the answer increases the validity and credibility of your findings. Watching yourself on video is one method to find your Blindspot – if you can drum up the courage to face the reality that video reveals. Combining video with the other strategies in this book – i.e. triangulation – is even more powerful.

References

Glassman, C. F. (2009). *Brain drain: The breakthrough that will change your life*. BookBaby.

Hamel, C., & Viau-Guay, A. (2019). Using video to support teachers' reflective practice: A literature review. *Cogent Education*, *6*(1), 1673689.

Hattie, J. (2023). *Visible learning: The sequel: A synthesis of over 2,100 meta-analyses relating to achievement*. Taylor & Francis.

Kostadinovska-Stojchevska, B., & Popovikj, I. (2019). Teacher talking time vs. student talking time: Moving from teacher-centered classroom to learner-centered classroom. *The International Journal of Applied Language Studies and Culture*, *2*(2), 25–31.

Kourieos, S. (2016). Video-mediated microteaching–A stimulus for reflection and teacher growth. *Australian Journal of Teacher Education*, *41*(1), 4.

McCoy, S., & Lynam, A. M. (2021). Video-based self-reflection among pre-service teachers in Ireland: A qualitative study. *Education and Information Technologies*, *26*(1), 921–944.

Morin, K. L., Ganz, J. B., Vannest, K. J., Haas, A. N., Nagro, S. A., Peltier, C. J., … & Ura, S. K. (2019). A systematic review of single-case research on video analysis as professional development for special educators. *The Journal of Special Education*, *53*(1), 3–14.

Further Reading

Brouwer, N. (2022). *Using video to develop teaching*. Routledge.

9

Self-Reflection

> We do not learn from experience; we learn from reflecting on experience. — John Dewey (1933)

Way, way back, when I was in teachers college, my pre-service teaching program was steeped in reflection. "Reflect, reflect, reflect" became a slogan that we, as teacher candidates, heard constantly. We were required to keep a reflection journal and to write in it every day. There were no particular prompts or instructions – we were simply told to reflect on the day and write down whatever we were thinking about. It didn't make much sense to me at the time. All this reflection – what was the point?

Now, decades later, I appreciate the wisdom. We were being initiated into a mindset: a reflective mindset, one extolled in education since John Dewey's groundbreaking book *How We Think* (1933), quoted above. We were developing the habit of taking the time to write our reflections down. And in my long teaching journey, I have noticed that the most effective teachers I encounter are the ones who have a reflection practice. They are the ones who keep a little notebook by their side and continually jot things down: questioning their work, trying out new things, and writing down their thoughts about the results.

Research supports this: Donald A. Schön (2017) examined five professions – engineering, architecture, management,

DOI: 10.4324/9781003490975-12

psychotherapy, and town planning – and discovered that within these professions, the habit of reflection separated the extraordinary professionals from mediocre ones. As in teaching, success in these fields relies less on formulas learned in school and more on the kind of understanding that is learned through experience and reflection. Researchers Bailey and Rehman, after interviewing 442 executives, discovered that being at the "top of your game" only comes when you "extract from your past how to engage the future." This requires regular, thoughtful, and deliberate reflection (Bailey & Rehman, 2022).

Schön distinguished between "reflection in action" and "reflection on action." "Reflection in action" is the thinking that happens when, in the moment, you think "That didn't go well, I wonder why, and what can I do about it, right now?" Also called "thinking on your feet" or "thinking while doing it," reflection-in-action reduces the chances of forgetting what actually happened. It allows teachers to improve their teaching immediately rather than waiting until the next opportunity (Beck and Kosnik, 2001).

A more deliberate approach involves reflecting back on events of the teaching day, analyzing where difficulties or challenges arose, considering options for overcoming them, and deciding on future actions (reflection on action). It involves diagnosis, evaluation, and intention-setting. Actively reflecting on past events allows teachers to fully embrace an experimental practice: trying things out, observing the results, and coming to conclusions about not just what was successful but why it was successful. Reflection helps teachers embrace an inquiry approach to their work (Çimer et al., 2013).

Writing makes reflection intentional. Research shows that self-reflection is most effective when it is captured in writing (e.g., Lew & Schmidt, 2011). Thoughts can be fleeting. Writing them down takes longer than thinking; therefore, it slows down the inner dialogue and forces us to stay with each thought for longer. It makes our thinking more purposeful, intentional, and focused. Writing also allows us to read back what we have written, to give us a more objective view of our thinking.

Making the time. Taking time for self-reflection is challenging in the context of your busy teaching day. It is tough to do when you have a pile of marking on your desk, emails to answer, and tomorrow's prep to take care of. However, even five minutes a day will yield long-term benefits.

Invest in a separate, small notebook and dedicate it to self-reflection about your practice. Before the teaching day begins, write down one thing that you are going to try doing differently, or one thing you want to be intentional about. It can be something small, such as writing the day's learning objective on the board, asking the question "What makes you say that?" in response to a student's comment, or using wait time more intentionally. Reflecting and writing down your intention will take about two minutes.

At the end of the teaching day, write a few sentences in response to that one thing: how did it work? How did your students respond? How might you tweak it going forward? Three minutes.

Keep your journal handy. Set an alarm for the time you will write the morning intention and another for the end-of-day reflection. When the alarm goes off, just do it.

Surprise, Frustration, Failure. In their research, Bailey and Rehman (2022) discovered that incidents that led to feelings of surprise, frustration, or failure were the most likely to yield significant personal growth when reflected upon. They recommend that you notice events, incidents, or interactions that surprise or frustrate you, as well as failures, and jot them down when they occur. The ones that result in an ***emotional*** response are the most valuable: reflect on how you felt – the pit in the stomach, the heaviness in the chest, the racing thoughts.

- **Surprise**: When something turned out differently than you had expected, this reveals that our understanding or assumptions were incorrect. Situations that surprise us are worth reflecting on, because we can then adjust the underlying misunderstandings.
- **Frustration**: We become frustrated when something we have planned or want is thwarted: our students get

pulled out of class for a sports tournament in the middle of an important lesson; the principal announces yet another educational initiative; six students in a row ask for a bathroom break. Moments of frustration became growth opportunities upon reflection, leading to other ways of coping with setbacks, such as patience, clearer communication, or better planning.

- **Failure**: Failure is a mistake made public: something about our thinking, judgments, or assumptions was mistaken and resulted in an observable fail. If we can reflect and pinpoint the source of the failure, then we will discover what *not* to do in the future.

At the end of the week, take a few minutes to review your notes. Add to them. Elaborate. What was it that made you feel the way you did? How did you contribute to the situation that surprised or frustrated you? What assumptions had you made that were incorrect? How do you need to adjust your thinking going forward?

Prompts for reflection. To further develop your self-awareness, you can pair this short-form reflection practice with a longer, weekly journaling exercise. Try scheduling in a half hour at the end of your work week to reflect on the week gone by. Some approaches that this longer form can take:

- ***What, so what, now what?*** This effective reflection tool was developed by Terry Borton in the '70s.
  - Step 1: "What" – identify and describe the event, experience, or situation as objectively as possible, without emotion or judgment. "Sandra, Ethan, and Emily continually made off-topic comments during class. This drew the other students' focus to them, and away from their work." You can use Bailey and Rehman's (2022) surprise, frustration, and failure to identify the moments worth exploring further.
  - Step 2: "So what" – describe the impact on you. This is where you dig into your feelings and emotions. "I was frustrated because they just wouldn't stop, even

when I asked them not to. I felt disrespected. Even a little bit angry."

- Step 3: "Now what" – write out possible solutions to improve the situation and prevent it from happening again. "I could: a) revisit the class rules with the entire class, b) pull those three aside for a private conversation, clarifying the consequences for such behavior, and/or c) change the seating arrangement." Make your plan, and carry it out. Identify what you have learned. (Borton, 1969)

◆ ***The 5-R framework for reflection.*** Developed by Bain et al. (1999, 2002), the 5-R framework lays out steps for long-form written reflection:

- **Reporting** of the context of the experience, in an objective, non-evaluative way. What happened? What did I do? Describe from a place of neutrality and non-judgment.
- **Responding** to the experience. Emotions, feelings, and thoughts: How did I feel? What was my gut reaction in the moment? What were my initial thoughts about the reasons that things happened the way they did?
- **Relating** the experience to knowledge and skills you already have. Have I seen this before? How is this the same or different from my prior experience?
- **Reasoning** about the significant factors to explain the experience. What research or literature can I read to help me here? How would someone who is knowledgeable about these types of situations respond?
- **Reconstructing** what happened so that in the future, I can deal with similar situations differently. What could I have done differently this time? How will I recognize a similar situation the next time it occurs? How can I respond differently then?

Bain et al. (1999, 2002) use the 5 Rs to evaluate the quality of reflections, suggesting that as you go down the list, the effectiveness of the written reflection increases.

◆ ***Byron Katie's "The Work."*** This in-depth approach created by Byron Katie (Katie, 2014) is tremendously helpful for reflecting on incidents, interactions, or events that have caused you emotional distress. A free PDF is available online that fully describes the process: (https://thework.com/wp-content/uploads/2019/02/English_LB.pdf). Briefly, *The Work* consists of reflecting on a judgmental thought that you have had that is upsetting to you. For example, "My students should listen to me when I'm speaking." You examine this thought by writing your response down to four questions:

- Is it true?
- Can I absolutely know that it is true?
- How does that thought make me feel?
- Who would I be without that thought?

Then you "turn around" the thought by writing it in its opposite form and finding examples of how this turned-around version could be true.

- A turnaround for "My student should listen to me when I'm speaking" is "My students ***shouldn't*** listen to me when I'm speaking." How is this true? Well, for starters, they are adolescents, and they are wired to attend to their peers more than to their elders – a bit of evolutionary psychology for you – see Judith Rich Harris's (2011) *The Nurture Assumption*.
- Another turnaround could be "***I*** should listen to ***them*** when they are speaking." How is this true? Well, I notice that I do most of the talking in the class, and perhaps I need to give them more opportunities to speak while I listen.

I notice that when I go through this written exercise and finish writing the turnarounds, it feels as if a huge weight has been lifted.

- ♦ **Three Wins of the Day**. Bailey and Rehman (2022) point out that reflection, done well, can be ego-bruising. Being honest with yourself can be hard. Think of it as eating your vegetables: good for you, but sometimes not your favorite thing. I recommend adding dessert: at the end of each day, identify three "wins" of the day and jot them down. This could be as simple as having a friendly interaction with a "difficult" student, speaking up at a staff meeting, or even getting to work on time (if this happens to be your personal challenge). Your wins are personal. If you are going to be your own coach, you also get to be your own cheerleader.

Finding your Blindspot. How will a practice of regular written reflection help you to identify your Blindspot? Well, this route is not as direct as the other strategies in this section. However, through reflection, we raise our self-awareness. The more self-aware we are, the more easily we can see ourselves honestly, flies and all. This opens us up to be able to receive information that we need, information that will help us to discern a Blindspot.

I have intentionally developed a habit of jotting down my thoughts at the beginning of each workday. I note down my intention for teaching that day. At 3:40, I put a check mark or a comment beside that intention. I also note down anything that surprised or frustrated me as well as any failures. And always, I write down my three wins of the day. On Fridays, I read over my notes and do a deep dive – an hour of writing – into something that had come up during the week. Something that surprised, frustrated, or left me with a sense of failure. Sometimes I follow Byron Katie's format. Sometimes I follow the 5 Rs. Sometimes I just free-write.

Over the last decade, as a result of this habit of regular self-reflection, I believe I have found that I have become more willing to admit my mistakes. I notice that I am more able to take responsibility for things that didn't go my way. I believe I am also getting better at receiving feedback. And, over time, I have begun to see things about myself that had previously been hidden – my tendency to be impulsive, for example, and for making last-minute changes. I also am better able to acknowledge my strengths: I can be creative, flexible, and responsive. In terms of the Classic 10, I know that I am a #5 (Get Organized), with #1 (Cut the Words) always needing attention. The good news is – I now know this, and I can work to improve upon it.

And so can you. Self-reflection is the path to self-awareness. Once you are aware of where you need to grow, you are ready for Part III of this book: strategies for addressing your Professional Practice Focus.

References

Bailey, J, & Rehman, S. (2022). Don't underestimate the power of self-reflection. *Harvard Business Review*.

Bain, J. D., Ballantyne, R., Mills, C., & Lester, N. C. (2002). *Reflecting on practice: Student teachers' perspectives*. Post Pressed.

Bain, J. D., Ballantyne, R., Packer, J., & Mills, C. (1999). Using journal writing to enhance student teachers' reflectivity during field experience placements. *Teachers and Teaching*, *5*(1), 51–73.

Beck, C. & Kosnik, C. (2001). Reflection-in-action: In defence of thoughtful thinking. *Curriculum Inquiry*, *31*(2), 217–227.

Borton, T. (1969). Reach, touch, and teach. *Saturday Rev*.

Çimer, A., Çimer, S. O., & Vekli, G. S. (2013). How does reflection help teachers to become effective teachers. *International Journal of Educational Research*, *1*(4), 133–149.

Dewey, J. (1933). *How We Think: A Restatement of the Relation of Reflective Thinking to the Educative Process*. D. C. Health.

Harris, J. R. (2011). *The nurture assumption: Why children turn out the way they do*. Simon and Schuster.

Katie, B. (2014). The Work of Byron Katie. *Eine Einführung*. https://thework.com/wp-content/uploads/2019/02/English_LB.pdf

Lew, D. N. M., & Schmidt, H. G. (2011). Writing to learn: can reflection journals be used to promote self-reflection and learning? *Higher Education Research & Development*, *30*(4), 519–532.

Schön, D. A. (2017). *The reflective practitioner: How professionals think in action*. Routledge.

Part III

You’ve Found Your Blindspot, So Now What?

10

What You Can Do About It

Knowing is half the battle. — Anonymous

Congratulations! You have identified your Blindspot. Like the quote (above), this is the hardest part. Once you are aware of it, acknowledge it, and are committed to addressing it, guess what? It is no longer a Blindspot. You can refer to it instead as your **Professional Practice Focus (PPF)**.

Identifying your PPF is by far the hardest part of the professional development journey. Now that you have found your Blindspot and have made this aspect of your practice a priority, you'll find that you naturally attend to fixing it. Simply being aware of the issue does go a very long way toward addressing it.

A key will be keeping your PPF in front of mind as you launch into your busy day-to-day life as a teacher. The more you can keep your attention on your PPF, the more you will develop it. Here are some ideas for maintaining your focus:

- Set a clear intention to focus on this aspect of your practice. Write it down. Post it on your computer or your agenda, somewhere visible that you will see throughout your day. However, research shows that humans quickly

DOI: 10.4324/9781003490975-14

habituate to visual cues (e.g., Ardiel et al., 2017), so you'll have to rewrite that post-it every day and stick it in a new place, or else it will quickly become just background "noise."

- Make a daily check-in or self-reminder about your PPF part of your morning routine. I use a chart I've made for myself (on Google Forms, using the checkbox function) listing all my daily, repeating work tasks – such as read the parent message app, set alarms, and check the school calendar. I also include a checkbox for writing down my morning intentions regarding my PPF. At the end of every day, I see how many "points" I get (using the =COUNTIF(C6:C54,TRUE) formula). Gamification works!
- At the end of each day, write about what you are learning and noticing related to your PPF in a journal.
- Seek out colleagues who also want to address this aspect of their practice. Consider forming a PLC (professional learning community). Arrange to meet regularly in a small group to share what you have been trying, what works, and what doesn't. Share resources. Support each other's efforts.
- Seek out colleagues who have strengths in your PPF and watch them teach. When I was working on PPF #7 (use every minute), I spent as much time as I could in Tony Araujo's classroom, observing his masterful way of keeping kids actively engaged from the minute they walked in the door to the minute they left the class. I learned more from watching him teach than any tip or trick I could find in a book or Pro-D session.
- If you feel comfortable, ask your principal or Director of Instruction for ideas, resources, and recommendations. Most school administrators will bend over backwards to support your professional development, especially if you have self-identified the issue you want to work on.
- The next chapter provides research-backed strategies, techniques, and the best resources I could find, listed by

PPF. These are meant to be starting points for you as you begin your journey. Don't read the entire chapter – just turn to your PPF and read that section. Try the strategies on for size. Seek out the resources. Dive in.
- If you feel comfortable, ask your school administrator to help you access the resources in the next chapter: your school may have a professional development budget for books. The articles you can source for free by searching them up in Google Scholar and clicking on the "pdf" version on the right-hand side of the page.

A caveat. The advice, strategies, and suggestions in the next chapter are meant to be used by a teacher who needs to address that particular Blindspot. **Do not** interpret all of this as general teaching advice. If you are a teacher who needs to Get Organized (PPF #6, for example), do **not** also try to Dial Back Overpreparation (PPF #4). This would be like adding salt to a dish that is already too salty!

And remember: Attend to one PPF at a time. Teaching is a complex, busy, important job. You have enough to do. If you want to make progress, you must focus your energy on one, and only one, PPF.

My advice is to find your Blindspot – the one area that will have a significant impact on your teaching (using Part II of this book) – and then focus on that one PPF for an entire school year – or at least a full term. When you feel like this has become an area of strength for you, you can go back and use the strategies in Part I to uncover your next priority. Think of it as ratcheting up a climbing wall – going from one rung to another to make slow, steady progress.

Some of these PPFs (e.g., PPF #1) can easily become a career-long focus. And that's okay! The goal is to be a better teacher … not a perfect one. Every step forward matters.

Feel good about having discovered what you need to work on. Know that the effort you put into developing this aspect of your practice is exactly what you need to become the best teacher you can be.

Reference

Ardiel, E. L., Yu, A. J., Giles, A. C., & Rankin, C. H. (2017). Habituation as an adaptive shift in response strategy mediated by neuropeptides. *NPJ Science of Learning*, *2*(1), 9.

11

Strategies for Addressing Your Professional Practice Focus

> It's the little details that are vital. Little things make big things happen. — John Wooden (1973)

Here are strategies, advice, techniques, and resources you can use to address your Professional Practice Focus (PPF). Please don't read this entire chapter – just skip to the PPF that you have identified as your needed focus.

Many of these ideas seem small, for example: writing a daily intention, remembering to breathe, tweaking the way you do one thing per day. But Coach Wooden, one of the world's most effective basketball coaches, made it clear: persistently and consistently attending to the small things adds up to big payoffs.

PPF #1: Cut the Words: Reduce Teacher Talk, Increase Student Talk

If you have identified Blindspot #1 as your PPF, you are in good company. In my experience, this is the most commonly occurring Blindspot. Why? Because (most) teachers love to talk. Addressing this PPF can transform your practice, leading to a more fully student-focused classroom. Research shows that in classrooms where the teacher talks less and where students

DOI: 10.4324/9781003490975-15

engage in higher rates and levels of student talk, students excel academically (Stichter et al., 2009) and engage in deeper learning (Hattie, 2023).

How to begin? Start simply by attending to your words. When you are aware of how much you talk in class, you will naturally find ways to be more concise and precise. You will also figure out strategies for having students do more of the talking.

Focus on how you give directions. This is a great first step for PPF #1. When you are giving instructions to your class (explaining what and how to do an upcoming task, for example), challenge yourself to deliver it in as few words as possible. Here are some strategies to try:

- Record (e.g., the voice app on your phone) yourself giving instructions. Later, transcribe what you said. Now re-write your verbal instructions in fewer words. This exercise trains you to say what you meant to say more precisely and concisely.
- Prior to giving instructions, write out what you are about to say. See if you can edit that down to fewer words. Then use your script when you address your class. Again, this is an exercise to try from time to time, to help you become more efficient – not something you should attempt to do every time.
- Be intentional about not repeating yourself. Say it once, say it well.

Regarding this last point, if you are going to say something only once, students need be able to hear you the first time. This means you must have their attention, quiet in the room, and eyes on you, ***before*** you speak.

- Use a signal if there is classroom noise (dinging a bell, clap-clap-clappity-clap, or asking students to "track me, please").
- Count down ("Track me in 5 – 4 – 3 – 2 – 1") to give students time to transition from activity time to listening time (Lemov, 2021).

- State the instructions clearly, concisely, and only once.
- Ask a student to repeat them back.
- Pair your verbal delivery with written instructions on the board or projected on the screen.
- If you are tempted to repeat any part of the instructions – don't. Repetition trains your students to not listen the first time (Linsin, 2009).
- If a student has a question about the instructions, reply "Great question. Can anyone else answer that?" Then allow another student to explain.

Obtain good data. "What gets measured gets improved." (quote attributed to Peter Drucker.) How do you measure the amount of teacher talk in your classroom?

- Sound-record a class. Later, listen to the playback while using a stopwatch to count and record the number of seconds you can hear your voice.
- (Less time-consuming for you) Have a colleague sit in your class with a stopwatch and a clipboard, recording the number of seconds you are speaking.
- Model to your students your desire to learn and grow as a teacher. Recruit a student to spend a class recording, with a stopwatch, the seconds you are speaking.

If you do this from time to time and then compare the minutes of teacher-talk time to total class time, you will find that you naturally cut back on your teacher talk. Because what gets measured naturally improves.

There are some apps (such as TeachFX and Visible Classroom) that will analyze the sound input from your class and give you fairly precise readings on the amount and proportion of teacher talk compared to student talk. These apps do come with a price tag, but the reviews seem to be overwhelmingly positive.

Develop skills to facilitate student voice. Reducing teacher talk increases opportunities for student talk. We want the students to do the heavy lifting in terms of explaining, justifying claims with evidence, critiquing ideas, and generally exercising their communicative and cognitive powers. So, while cutting back on teacher talk, work on acquiring tools to develop your students' willingness and ability to use ***their*** voices productively. This includes fostering students' ability to listen carefully to their peers and to build on or critique their peers' thinking.

- Move away from the IRE pattern so common in classrooms. IRE stands for Initiation (teacher asks a question) – Response (student responds) – Evaluation (teacher confirms whether the answer is correct or not). Evaluation from the teacher tends to close down the conversation. The emphasis is on correctness rather than reasoning (see Michaels & O'Connor, 2015). Instead, reconceptualize classroom discussion as student to student to student, with the teacher facilitating and encouraging all students' voices in higher-level discussion.
- **Use wait time effectively**. Your students need time to think. When you train yourself to use wait time effectively, you engage the students who need more time to process before responding verbally. This will go a long way toward including more student voices in classroom discussion.
- Provide **sentence starters** (e.g., "Jamal's point about X was important because …").
    - Post sentence starters on the wall or give each student a laminated card with a selection of sentence starters.
    - Practice using sentence starters with your students. Conduct a conversation about something trivial, such as "the best ice-cream flavor," requiring each student to begin their contribution with one of the sentence starters. Then progress to more substantial topics.
    - See Appendix A for sentence starter ideas appropriate by grade level.
- Redirect students' comments away from the teacher and toward each other. Use a visual signal (e.g., pointing to other students' eyes) to remind students to look at each other, not the teacher when they are responding to each other's comments.
- Teach students to "track" the speaker: i.e., turn your body and use your eyes to look at whomever is speaking. You

can cue this by simply saying "Track Ella, please" before Ella speaks. This creates a culture of support and appreciation for the student speaking (Lemov, 2021).

- Train students to signal their agreement with the speaker non-verbally (thumbs up, a "hang ten" hand sign, or a rocking fist). This encourages the speaker without the need to interrupt with verbalized agreement.
- Employ partner talk (e.g., "think-pair-share") to increase every student's access to talking time.
- Rather than responding to student's contributions with an evaluation (e.g., "that's correct"), use a "talk tool" – a teacher response that will elicit student voice. For example:
  - "Can you say more about that?"
  - "Can anyone add on to the idea that Aiden has raised?" or
  - "Who can explain in their words why Naomi said that?"
  - See Appendix B for Nine Talk Moves you can use to develop student voice and student thinking, adapted from Michaels and O'Connor (2015).
- To further transition your classroom from teacher voice–focused to student voice– and student thinking–focused, consider exploring related pedagogical approaches:
  - The Harkness Method. This is an approach to teaching developed at Phillips Exeter Academy in New Hampshire, resembling a Socratic seminar. Students sit around a large oval table, where student-led discussions drive the learning. Students learn to engage in self-regulated group discussions, inquiry, collaboration, and critical thinking. The resulting discussions entirely replace teacher talk. Training in the method is available at Exeter Academy (https://www.exeter.edu/programs-educators/harkness-outreach).
  - Thinking Classrooms. In mathematics, this looks like students standing up at the whiteboard and, working out problems in small groups, rather than the teacher at the front of the class showing them how. In a Thinking Classroom, most of the talking is done by the students

in their groups as they collaborate to figure things out. See Peter Liljedahl's excellent book *Building Thinking Classrooms in Mathematics, K-12* (Corwin).

- The Jigsaw Method. Working in groups, individual students within the group are assigned subtopics of a larger topic. They research and develop their understanding of the subtopic, and then teach it to the rest of the group. In the teaching phase, group members ask questions to clarify their understanding, provide feedback, and work collectively to build shared understanding. In Hattie's Visible Learning work (2023), the Jigsaw Method had an effect size of 1.2, the highest of all the teaching methods studied using meta-analysis. See https://www.jigsaw.org/overview/ for more about the method.
- Spider Web Discussion. Like the Harkness method, this approach teaches students to engage in student-led discussions by shifting the teacher's role from central character to coach and observer. See Alexis Wiggins's *The Best Class You Never Taught* (ASCD, 2017). (The title refers to the fact that this method results in less teacher talk.)

◆ **Listen to your students**. When you are speaking with a student one-on-one, give them your full attention. Few kids ever have the luxury of full attention from an adult. Put your agenda on the back burner and listen to them. Take your time before responding – and think twice before changing the topic, supplying your ideas, or telling them they are mistaken. Be curious and open, and **let them talk**. Allowing students to use their voice is often far more valuable than you using yours.

Further Reading

Boryga, A. (2023, January 9). *Small shifts to limit 'Teacher talk' and increase engagement.* Edutopia. https://www.edutopia.org/article/limit-teacher-talk-increase-student-engagement-achievement/

Burkins, J., & Yaris, K. (2023). *Who's doing the work?: How to say less so readers can do more*. Routledge.

Tovani, C., & Moje, E. B. (2017). *No more telling as teaching: Less lecture, more engaged learning*. Heinemann.

Wiggins, A. (2017). *The best class you never taught: How spider web discussion can turn students into learning leaders*. ASCD.

Apps for AI-Assisted Voice Analysis in the Classroom

Visible Classroom. https://kb.ai-media.tv/knowledge-base/how-does-visible-classroom-work/

Teach FX. https://teachfx.com

PPF #2: Correct Verbal Hazards

Your speaking voice is personal and habitual. Changing that is hard. However, if you have learned that something about your speaking voice is impeding your credibility, your students' learning, or both, then it's worth the effort to make a change. The good news is that if you are aware that, in your classroom, your voice is not producing the effects that you would like, you are halfway there.

To actively address the issue, consider the following:

- Healthy vocal production requires good posture. Stand tall, arms and legs uncrossed, and think of fully occupying your space. Ground your stance by putting weight equally on two feet.
- Breathe before speaking and focus on the exhale as you speak. Think of breathing low rather than from your chest.
- Ensure that you are facing the class when you speak. For example, don't talk while writing on the whiteboard, as your back is turned to the class. Even if you twist around to speak, your posture will be compromised. Wait until you have finished writing. Then turn and face the class to speak.

- Stand relatively still to speak. Too much movement while speaking makes it difficult for students to focus their attention and process what you are saying. You do not need to stay rooted to one spot – you should, as a teacher, be moving about the classroom, but aim to move in the silences between your sentences.
- Hydrate! Good vocal production requires hydrated vocal cords.
- The larger the room, the slower you need to speak, as your voice will reverberate around the room.

"What gets measured gets improved." Peter Drucker's famous quote applies here.

- Set a sound recorder up, record a class, and later listen to the playback. When you hear your particular vocal challenge, you will automatically adjust the way you speak. And yes, I know how awful it is to listen to the sound of your own voice – but try to focus on the thing you are trying to address. Remember: developing self-awareness takes courage. You can do hard things.
- This next suggestion is for the truly courageous: enlist your students. If, for example, your particular vocal hazard is using the same word or phrase too often, then assign a student (one – not all!) to tally your use of that repetitive peccadillo. Collect your score at the end of class. Watch your score decline day after day. Bonus: When you tell your class that you are working on improving your teaching and that you need their help, you have modelled a growth mindset, humility, and trust. This is truly a win-win all around.

The following are suggestions for various types of verbal hazards, to help you address the one that is yours:

- Baby voice. Start by understanding your intention behind using a tone of voice that is too young for your students. My guess is that you wish to sound friendly and relatable. There are better ways of doing this – ways that are less likely to make your students feel talked down to. Remember that children and adolescents want to be thought of as capable and respected. Focus instead on using the same ***tone*** of voice you would use to address someone your age, adjusting the ***content*** so that it is age-appropriate.

- Kidspeak. As with baby voice, be aware that while your intention may be to be perceived by students as warm and relatable, using kidspeak too often may undermine your credibility. Identify the expressions you regularly use that sound inappropriately young. McWhorter (2019) provides some examples:
  - Childish use of the word *because*: "I believe in climate change because … science" and "I'm cleaning my room because ... procrastination."
  - Use of the phrase "All the things" as in "We're going to do all the things!" or "I've had all the illnesses."
  - Intentional mispronunciations on purpose, such as "feets" for "feet," "Dis" for "this," or "pacifically" instead of "specifically."
  - Filler word use such as "I mean," "you know," "like," "and stuff like that," to soften the meaning of what you are saying.

  When you raise your awareness and are conscious of your intentions, you will begin to notice when you are using kidspeak. When you notice, simply stop, take a breath, and correct yourself. Remind yourself that you are the adult in the room, and that students need to be able to respect you as an adult, not connect to you as a peer.
- Uptalk. If you find yourself using uptalk, also known as upspeak or high rising terminal (HRT), then your declarative sentences can sound like questions, thanks to a habitual rise in the pitch at the end. You may intend to sound invitational and inclusive, but in fact, many speech experts agree that users of uptalk sound uncertain and lacking in confidence (Warren, 2016). It can lead your students to doubt what you are saying, question your

leadership, or (worst of all) adopt the habit for themselves. You do not want your students heading out into the world using uptalk inappropriately.

Another version of uptalk is a too-frequent use of "OK?" when giving instructions. "You're going to choose three colors, OK? Then color in the round shapes red, OK?" This has the same effect as uptalk: it is intended to make the speaker sound inclusive and inviting, but instead can make the speaker sound insecure and lacking in confidence.

Use of uptalk is a habit that you can change if you want to. Start by understanding your motivation for using it in the first place. Then engage in regular, deliberate practice: write out some instructions that you intend to give to your class. Practice speaking them out loud in front of the mirror, paying close attention to the ends of your sentences. Like any new behavior, this may feel awkward at first but will feel increasingly more natural over time. Sound-recording yourself and listening to playback are great ways to get feedback on your progress.

- **Use of repetitive words or phrases**. I will admit that when I was a student musician, I had a conductor who used the word "fabulous!" so often that we used to tally the number of times he said the word and compare notes after rehearsal. The day he hit "fabulous" for the 40th time in a two-hour rehearsal, we all cheered. Clearly, we weren't paying attention to what we should have been doing (listening to his instructions and feedback). The moral of this story: overuse of a word or phrase can be distracting. Your students may stop listening to what you are actually saying.

  Actively listen to yourself when you speak. Once you know you have a habit of overusing a go-to expression, you'll likely catch yourself before saying it. Slowing down your speech and being more deliberate will help. Don't fear the silence: it's okay to pause while you think of the best words to use.

Set measurable goals for reducing the repetitive phrase from your speech, such as going an entire class without using it. Set up a recording device (aka your phone) beside you and record yourself. Listen to the playback: if your go-to word is absent, give yourself a reward!

Recruit your students. Tell them to give you a signal (e.g., raise your arm straight up and give a finger-wave) if they hear you say the word or phrase. Bonus: when you tell your students that you wish to become a better teacher and need their help to improve, you are modelling lifelong learning and a growth mindset.

- **Overuse of the first-person plural when it isn't appropriate**. You are a teacher. It is expected that you will give your students instructions and directions. You don't need to mask them as something else. Acting as if "we're all in this together" by announcing "we are going to write our name at the top of the page," when what you mean is "Please write your name at the top of the page," runs the risk of sounding insincere.

  Again, self-awareness is the key. Once you intend to change the way you speak to your students, you will naturally improve. Write out the instructions you intend to give vocally and practice reading them out loud. This will help you to adapt to your new way of speaking more easily.
- **Speaking with a shrill or too-loud tone of voice**. Teachers who use a too-shrill or too-loud tone of voice are responding to a need to be heard over student noise. Instead, develop tools to gain students' attention, wait for silence, and then speak in a clear voice, just loud enough to be heard at the back of the class.

  Examples of attention-getters:
  - Clap-in pattern. The ubiquitous "clap – clap – clap-clap-clap" is classic for a reason: it works. You can vary it by following with "clap – snap – clap-clappy-clap" and other rhythmic patterns until everyone has joined in, has stopped talking, and is facing you, ready to listen.

- High five. Raise your arm straight above your head and wave from just your fingers. Teach your students that when you do this, they are to stop talking, copy you, and give you their attention. When everyone has an arm straight up and is waving just their fingers, they are ready to listen.
- Instrumental. Play a "bing-bing-bing" on a tiny xylophone or some other high-pitched (easily heard above the throng) instrument. Train your students to respond quickly by stopping what they are doing and giving you their attention.
- Pitch matching. (A favorite of choir teachers everywhere.) Sing "oooooo" in a higher-pitched tone. Students are to match your pitch by singing the same note. It takes only moments for everyone to be singing "ooooo" – they cannot sing and talk at the same time – at which point you can use a conductor's cut-off gesture to stop the sound. Now you have their attention.

These attention-getters work only if you explicitly teach your students how they should respond to the cue. Practice, practice again, and celebrate when they are successful. Then, when you do have their attention, speak with a confident, warm, tone. Experiment with how quietly you can speak and still be heard. You'll be surprised – and the more quietly you speak, the more your students will hang onto your every word.

◆ **Speaking in a monotone, lacking presence, or otherwise employing a sleep-inducing delivery**. Teachers need to use vocal variation to keep their students engaged. If you have identified this as your Blindspot (now your PPF), then you are going to have to get out of your comfort zone! Varying vocal pitch and speaking more expressively can feel very awkward if you are used to speaking in a flat style.

Practice speaking with over-the-top dramatic flair in private – away from your students. Read out loud, overdoing the expression, and record yourself doing it.

Children's stories are great for this kind of practice: you can experiment with different voices – scary, bossy, frightened, jubilant. Overdo it! This will stretch your range and add flexibility to your delivery. When you get back to the front of your class, pull back, and just focus on speaking with a warm and expressive tone.

- **Speaking too quickly, with too little space between phrases**. Students need time to absorb what you are saying. If you speak too quickly, students will miss parts of what you are saying and they will feel anxious as a result of your frantic pace. And you will exhaust yourself.

  If your first language is not English and the rate of your native language is inherently faster, you may be unknowingly speaking English at the rate of your first language. This can heighten the effect of any accent you may have, making it that much more difficult for students to comprehend what you are saying.

  The solution to fast-talking? Breathe. Take time to inhale, take time to exhale. Feel your breath low in your body. Breathwork will calm you down, slow you down, and force you to insert breaks into your speech.

  Try this: after every sentence that you speak, stop, and repeat the sentence you just said, silently in your head. This may feel incredibly awkward, but it allows time for the meaning to sink in. Alternatively, after you finish every sentence, and before you begin the next, repeat a short, silent mantra such as "I am calm" or "I am poised."

  Practice speaking slowly at home, in private. Read out loud. Speak even more slowly than you think is reasonable. Take longer pauses. Then when you speak to your class, you will naturally speed up from too slow to a reasonable speed.

  Elicit your students' help: Tell them that you are a fast talker, and you need them to let you know if they need you to slow down. You could even pre-arrange a visual signal that they can give you, such as rolling their hands, to indicate that you're going too fast. This is an excellent opportunity for your students to practice self-advocacy.

Your speaking voice has an enormous effect on your students' behavior, attitude, and learning (Paulmann & Weinstein, 2023). With some courage, commitment, and lots of practice, you can develop a teacher voice that elicits respect and rapport from your students and keeps them engaged and connected to their learning.

Further Reading

DeVore, K., & Cookman, S. (2020). *The voice book: Caring for, protecting, and improving your voice*. Chicago Review Press.

Douglas, H. (2021, December 11). How to use your teacher voice to transform behaviour overnight. *Medium*. https://medium.com/age-of-awareness/make-the-most-of-your-teacher-voice-d9b4b0655109

Martin, S., & Darnley, L. (2017). *The voice in education: Vocal health and effective communication*. Compton Publishing Ltd.

Terada, Y. (2023, April 14). *How tone of voice shapes your classroom culture*. Edutopia. https://www.edutopia.org/article/how-tone-of-voice-shapes-your-classroom-culture

PPF #3: Loosen the Reins: Stop Micromanaging – Students Are More Capable than You Think

If you have identified "loosening the reins" as your PPF, the solution is to focus on supporting student autonomy and agency.

Research shows that directly controlling teacher behaviors (DCTBs) predict poor motivation and engagement in K-12 students (Assor et al., 2005). According to the researchers, DCTBs explicitly attempt to fully and instantly change children's behaviors or the opinions they hold. Examples are

- giving frequent directives (micromanaging),
- not allowing children to voice opinions that differ from those expressed by the teacher,

- not letting children work at their preferred pace,
- not permitting student choice or preferences in situations where there is no good reason not to.

(Assor et al., 2005)

Autonomy-supportive teacher behaviors, on the other hand, that predict better academic and emotional outcomes include:

- the provision of choice,
- explanation of relevance, and
- acceptance of criticism.

(Reeve & Cheon, 2021)

Face your fears. If this is your PPF, you may feel that if you loosen your grip, you will lose control of your class. If you have had that classic teacher's nightmare that you are teaching in your underwear, it might mean that deep down, losing control is a lurking fear. As motivational speaker Tim Ferriss puts it, "Fear comes in many forms, and we usually don't call it by its four-letter name" (Ferriss, 2017). In other words, fear can translate into controlling behaviors without your realizing it.

It may help you to write in a journal about your feelings about allowing students more autonomy and agency. Write about the worst-cast scenario, playing out the "what-ifs" out on paper. You may find that facing your fears in this way reduces their impact.

Know that well-established classroom routines, clear expectations, and consistent consequences are the bedrock of classroom management. If these are in place, you can afford to explore autonomy-supportive teaching behaviors.

Making the shift starts with your attitude. Are you student-focused or self-focused during your teaching day? (Vansteenkiste et al., 2019). Autonomy-supportive teachers have a curious, open, and flexible attitude toward students. They take an interest in students' emerging interests and preferences (Reeve & Cheon, 2021). In short, they take the students' perspective. Begin to shift your focus from what ***you*** need to what your ***students*** are experiencing, moment to moment.

An interesting survey tool that researchers have used to determine teachers' level of autonomy-supportive behaviors asks students to rate their agreement with statements, such as

- "I think [teacher's name] will let kids do things their own way"
- "My teacher lets me make decisions"
- "My teacher is interested in my ideas"
- "I think [teacher's name] will try to control everything"

(Gurland & Evangelista, 2015)

The goal, then, is to find ways to behave so that your students would answer "yes" to the first three questions and "no" to the fourth. Think about what you can do – the small moments, the brief student–teacher interactions – that will support students' sense of autonomy and agency. Here are some places to start:

Offer choice. Where you can, offer choice. The less you can dictate exactly how things must be done, the more opportunities your students will have to develop their autonomy. Does their name really have to go in the top right-hand corner of the paper? Or is it sufficient that their name is printed clearly on the paper so that you can tell to whom it belongs? Do they need to share their learning in a PowerPoint presentation? Or can they choose another mode of presentation, such as a podcast? Would they like to practice this particular skill one more time, or would they like to move on?

There are times you cannot offer choice: students cannot choose to adhere to safety precautions. They shouldn't choose whether or not to do their best work. They don't have the choice to be respectful or not. In these situations, explain the reasons why you are asking them to do these things.

Offer rationale. We often have to ask students to do things that they feel are uninteresting, arbitrary, or meaningless. For example, requesting that students be silent during fire drills, asking them to double-check their work, making them practice math facts, or requiring them to cite their sources: if they do not understand these requests, students may see them as arbitrary acts of teacher dominance.

The solution? Explain the reasons for requests in terms of how this activity will be useful to them. Reveal the "hidden value" and "personal relevance" within the request (Vansteenkiste et al., 2018). For example: practicing math facts will make problem-solving in math so much easier. If we take turns speaking, rather than all talking at once, it means that everyone in the room can be heard. If we stay silent during fire-drills, it is more likely that we will be able to stay silent if the real thing occurs – and thus be able to hear important, life-saving instructions.

Demonstrate to students that their opinions and perspectives are valued (Gurland & Evangelista, 2015). When your students are speaking, listen to them closely. Don't be quick to correct their thinking, share your knowledge, or offer your view. Active listening (nodding, eye-contact, asking clarifying questions) indicates that you value their perspective.

When you have the opportunity to say "yes" to your students' ideas or proposals, say "yes." Reflect on your knee-jerk responses: if your tendency is to say "no," challenge yourself to find a way to "yes." An automatic "no" can feel dismissive and controlling and can cost your students' their sense of autonomy.

Give students reasonable latitude to be in charge of their behavior. Let them handle tasks that they're capable of handling. Let them figure it out. You don't need to hover.

Do not repeat instructions: get your students into the habit of listening the first time. Yes, they may make mistakes, they may get it wrong, but it's okay. That's how we learn.

You can tell students 15 times to keep back from the edge of the shallow pond; or you can tell them once. If they stray, fall in, and get their feet wet, then, well, they get their feet wet. It is worse to harangue, eroding their sense that they are a whole human being, capable of making decisions, and capable of learning from mistakes.

Experiment. Take an experimental approach. Dial back the extent to which you direct students (within appropriate levels for the age group you teach) and see what happens. Keep it age-appropriate, take small risks, and notice the effects of loosening a little. You may loosen too much and need to adjust back. This is okay – this is all part of tweaking your level of control. But simply knowing that there is such a thing as too much control is Step 1 – and a significant step – toward growth in this area.

Look for opportunities to demonstrate autonomy-supportive behaviors. The teaching day is full of moments, big and small, when you can adjust the way you relate to your students. It can be helpful to keep a journal to record your efforts. At the end of the day, write down a short description of each moment you intentionally chose an autonomy-supportive behavior: a time you listened carefully to a student without interrupting or instructing. A time you provided choice. A time you said "yes" to a student idea or initiative. A time you gave instructions once and then let them complete the task without additional input from you. By intentionally attending to these moments, noting them, and celebrating small victories, you will find that your need for control relaxes.

The good news. Research shows that autonomy-supportive teaching styles are linked to teacher social and emotional well-being (Siacor et al., 2023). Feel better *and* prevent burnout, all while developing students' agency and autonomy. Sounds like a win-win.

Further Reading

Hayhurst, J., & DeRosa, J. (2021). *WIRE for agency | Four simple moves that transfer learning | Professional development book for educators | Grade Level K-5*. Benchmark Education Company.

Reeve, J. (2009). Why teachers adopt a controlling motivating style toward students and how they can become more autonomy supportive. *Educational Psychologist, 44*(3), 159–175.

Reeve, J. (2016). Autonomy-supportive teaching: What it is, how to do it. In *Building autonomous learners: Perspectives from research and practice using self-determination theory* (pp. 129–152). Springer Singapore. http://ndl.ethernet.edu.et/bitstream/123456789/41621/1/636.Ai-Girl%20Tan.pdf#page=143

Reeve, J., & Cheon, S. H. (2021). Autonomy-supportive teaching: Its malleability, benefits, and potential to improve educational practice. *Educational Psychologist, 56*(1), 54–77.

Vaughn, M. (2021). *Student agency in the classroom honoring student voice in the curriculum*. Teachers College Press.

PPF #4: Dial Back Over-Preparation

As I explained in Chapter 2, if over-preparation is the chink in your armor, it can show up in two ways: lack of work–life balance and inflexibility in teaching. To risk repeating myself: I am not advocating under-preparation. Teachers need to prepare their lessons, full stop. But, if you *over*-plan, it can get in the way of your ability to respond flexibly to student cues, student interests, and student feedback.

If a tendency to over-prepare has been identified as your personal quagmire, then you need to attend to this on two fronts: managing anxiety and developing your flexibility in response to student needs.

Managing anxiety. It can be terrifying to walk into class and willingly embrace the discomfort of not knowing exactly what you are going to be doing every minute of class. Those meticulous PowerPoint presentations that you prepared over the weekend can provide a lot of comfort. They show you exactly what to do, slide by slide. The worksheets you have planned, the preformed questions, the step-by-step lesson – these all go a long way toward calming you down and helping you to feel in control. The problem is that they can mask your ability to see what your students need – in the moment.

So you need tools *other* than preparation to help you manage the anxiety that comes with facing a room full of young learners. (I don't care if they are five years old or 17, a big group of learners can be intimidating!) Start with the number one anxiety queller: breathing.

Breathing. Just being aware of your breathing goes a long way toward relaxing your mind and body. Take some time – even a few seconds – to notice where you feel your breath. Feel the sensation of the inhale and exhale inside your nostrils. Observe the rise and fall of your chest and your abdomen. Can you feel the breath in your back? Don't try to adjust the way you breathe – just notice it.

You can check in with your breathing while sitting at your desk, while standing waiting for your class to arrive, even when walking from the staffroom to your classroom. I like to check in with my breathing while waiting at the photocopier for copies to run through. Try to take these mindful breathing moments multiple times throughout the day.

For an even more powerful calming technique, take a deep inhale through your nostrils while counting silently for two seconds, hold your breath for two seconds, then slowly exhale for four seconds, focusing on the sensation of your breath. Again, you can do this anywhere – during staff meetings, while on recess duty, when walking to the principal's office for your annual review.

Meditation, yoga, or other mindfulness training done at home or off-site can help you access a calmer state throughout your work day. You can find free guided meditations online (e.g., https://ggia.berkeley.edu/practice/mindful_breathing). Check out apps like Headspace and Ten Percent Happier. They cost a little but are absolutely worth it if you can commit to using them regularly.

Mindset. The tendency to over-plan may result from a perfectionist mindset. Many perfectionists have a fear-based orientation: rather than hoping for the best, they strive to avoid the worst. Anything short of a flawless performance is simply not good enough.

And this is the issue: if you over-focus on your *own* performance, then your focus is misplaced. It needs to be on the students. Now, obviously, the purpose of planning is to create excellent learning experiences for your students – but there is no way you can predict or control the moment-to-moment student responses to your every move. Trying to prep your way to perfection will simply exhaust you and get in your way.

The antidote to perfectionism is **flexibility**. Remember that both Berliner (2008) and Hattie (2023), in their extensive research on excellence in teaching, found that "Experts are more opportunistic and flexible in their teaching" (Hattie, p. 6). The ability to shift directions in response to students' questions, student needs in the moment, and student interests – this is what needs to take the place of over-planning and over-preparing.

Easier said than done. I know. But first, let me be clear: We're not talking about throwing all your plans out the window and letting students run the show. I'm not suggesting you show up to class and say, "What do you want to do today?" and go with whatever they suggest (with my students, that would be watching YouTube). We're talking about a slight shift ***in the direction of*** letting go: loosening your grip on controlling everything that happens in the classroom. Allowing your teaching to ***respond*** to your students rather than imposing upon them.

Here is an example. In a grade 8 English class preparing to study a Shakespeare play, students need to know what iambic pentameter is. Over-preparation might consist of the teacher creating and then delivering a lengthy, detailed PowerPoint presentation that explains what an iamb is, what pentameter is, and gives a long, technical explanation of how iambic pentameter works, followed by a variety of examples. Students then work on a worksheet that has them circling iambs in the text, marking stressed and unstressed syllables, identifying iambic pentameter, and rewriting sentences to craft sets of five iambs. Nice. And a lot of work to prepare the slideshow and worksheet plus an entire class period to cover the material and the exercise.

Alternatively, you

- Tell students as simply as possible what the concept is: Iambic pentameter is the rhythm that sounds like this: ba-dum, ba-dum, ba-dum, ba-dum, ba-dum. Count each iamb with your fingers.
- Demonstrate the concept: Recite: 'So **foul** and **fair** a **day** I **have** not **seen**' (Macbeth 1:3) out loud. Have students count the five "ba-dums" on their fingers. How many? Five. Iambic (ba-dum) pentameter (five).
- Provide a counterexample: Recite: 'I **heard** a **fly** buzz **when** I **died**' from Emily Dickenson's poem of the same name. Tell students to count the iambs on their fingers. How many ba-dums? Four. Not iambic pentameter.
- Provide another counterexample: Recite: '**Just** for a **hand**ful of **sil**ver he **left** us; **Just** for a **rib**and to **stick** in his **coat**' from Robert Browning's poem *The Lost Leader*. How many ba-dums? None. The rhythm isn't ba-dum, ba-dum, ba-dum, but long-short-short, long-short-short. So, not iambic.

- Have students distinguish between examples and counterexamples: Read a few more examples. Ask students to close their eyes and indicate with a thumbs-up if the poem uses iambs and then to hold up fingers for the number of iambs. This gives you real-time feedback on whether or not they understand the concept.

In 10 minutes – give or take – students now understand the concept. All you need is a handful of examples and counterexamples – no PowerPoints or worksheets required. And the rest of the class time can be used for other productive work.

Note the emphasis on what students already know, what students can contribute themselves, and what students can figure out on their own or in collaboration. There is less emphasis on teacher pre-prepared materials, teacher-imposed learning, and teacher control of the pace. The teacher's actions ***are in response*** to the students rather than in response to a pre-crafted plan and pre-prepared materials.

You will need to experiment. Try being less prepared with just one class. Go in with a general idea of the concept you are going to teach, have an idea of various ways you could approach it, and then focus in on your students' responses to what you are doing. Do they get it right away? Should you move faster? Are they engaged? Do they need you to slow down and go over a concept again?

Embrace improvisation. The word "improvisas" refers to something which cannot be foreseen in advance (Montuori, 2017). In the context of teaching, Professional Improvisation (PI) refers to *simultaneous decision and action within a pedagogical setting* (Ben-Horin, 2016) – in other words, departure from a pre-planned teaching sequence. Embraced by more progressive teacher education programs, PI is meant to produce learning experiences which happen as a result of interaction. Fully responding to students through PI contributes to their perception of being seen and heard.

One way to approach PI is to think of pulling things out of your toolbox in response to students and situations. This does mean you need to have a fully stocked toolbox – that is, a broad repertoire of activities, examples, techniques, and stories that you can pull out in an instant. Work on building up this toolbox as your foundation.

Be intentionally responsive. Shift your mindset from imposing learning on the students (these are the things that they will do, the text they will read, the questions they will answer, the activities they will engage in) to responding ***to*** the students. What do they already know? What are they curious about?

This requires you to continuously "read the room" and understand from your students' perspective what they are experiencing, what they need, and how they are learning. Continuously **check for understanding**. This ongoing "checking in" can look like this:

- Circulating through the room as students work;
- Frequently asking questions on the fly;
- Ask students for a thumbs up/thumbs down to indicate if they understand or not;
- Ask students for a four-finger rating (1 = I don't understand; 2 = I'm still a little confused; 3 = I understand and can do it by myself; 4 = I can teach a friend)
- Use exit tickets – students jot down an answer to a check-for-understanding question as they leave the room;
- Mini whiteboards: students write down a short answer to a question on an individual whiteboard and hold it up for you to see.
- The KWL strategy: students fill in a chart (Know – Want to know – Learned) to document prior understanding (K), create questions to motivate their learning (W), and after the learning activity, engage in reflection about their learning (L) (Ogle, 1986).

When you have better information about how your students are doing, you will be able to modify instruction in response. And this is the value of loosening a practice of watertight planning.

Further Reading

Biesta, G. J. (2015). *Beautiful risk of education*. Routledge.

Fisher, D., & Frey, N. (2014). *Checking for understanding: Formative assessment techniques for your classroom*. ASCD.

Fletcher-Wood, H. (2018). *Responsive teaching: Cognitive science and formative assessment in practice*. Routledge.

Sawyer, R. K. (2004). Creative teaching: Collaborative discussion as disciplined improvisation. *Educational researcher*, *33*(2), 12–20.

Sawyer, R. K. (2011). *Structure and improvisation in creative teaching*. Cambridge University Press.

Storm, A. (2023, August 14). *KWL Chart Teaching & Learning Strategy: Examples, templates, and other strategies*. Thinkific. https://www.thinkific.com/blog/kwl-chart-teaching-learning-strategy/

PPF #5. Get Organized: Provide Students with Clarity, Consistency, and Accountability

There are mountains of resources out there to help you get organized. You can invest any amount of your own money in shelving, bins, color-coding, labels, filing systems, beautiful planners, and so on. At the end of the day, however, your efforts at organization need to result in improved clarity, consistency, and accountability for students.

The reason to get organized is so your students know what to expect in your classroom. It means you need a classroom set up for success, classroom routines, clear communication about learning objectives, and clarity around assessment.

Classroom set-up. A cluttered, disorganized classroom sends the strong, unspoken message that a careless, haphazard, and good-enough effort is acceptable. Piles of papers, cluttered countertops, old student projects piled up in the corner, messy desktops – all this distracts from learning, sets a bad example, and communicates mediocrity.

On the other hand, you do not need to spend your time and money creating an overly pretty space that will win likes on Instagram. In Michael Linsin's words, "Never fall into the trap of believing that adorable, magical, and whimsical design, cutesy creative organization, or lamps and bean bag chairs have anything to do with good teaching. Mostly, they're a giant red flag" (Linsin, 2022). Focus on simplicity, order, and clarity.

Students learn best when they are not distracted. Put your energy into making the space neat, simple, and functional. Students need to know where to find what they need. Pens, papers, calculators, and so on should have a place and be returned to that place after use. Students should know exactly where to hand things in, how to retrieve marked papers, and where to keep their belongings. Figure it out, set it up, and stay consistent.

Classroom routines. Part of getting organized is developing classroom routines that are clear, fair, and non-negotiable. You must explicitly teach them to students and then practice them, just like fire drills. And then continue to reinforce them throughout the year. But when they're in place and working, routines free you and your students from endless navigation and wasted time throughout the rest of the year.

I can't tell you what your classroom routines should be. This will depend entirely upon what, where, and whom you are teaching.

- My beginning band students learn right from Day 1 that they are to set up the chairs and music stands before opening their instrument case. I explicitly teach them that they are to put their instrument together and sit practicing silent fingerings while they wait for the class to begin. They play their first notes only when I indicate that it's time to play. I teach these routines on the first day of class, and it saves me from repeating the same instructions over and over.
- Students in my grade 7 humanities class know to bring their ABC (agenda, binder, Chromebook) to class every

day. They know there will be a "Do Now" written on the board so that when they enter the class they know exactly what to do. When I remind them to "STAR", they know to Sit up, Track the speaker, Appreciate the speaker, and Respect the speaker – whether the speaker is me or one of their colleagues. (The STAR routine is from Lemov, 2021).

- Routines for my grade 11 Economic Theory course, however, are very different. The nature of the learning, the maturity of the students, and the physical space require different routines. This group needs routines for discussion protocols, handing in papers, and ways to catch up if they are absent from a class.

To work out what routines you need for your teaching context, Do a brain-dump and write down everything that occurs regularly in your classroom, such as when students enter the room, students pass out supplies, students hand in papers, students go to the bathroom. Work out how to handle each of these efficiently and effectively in your classroom. Invest time at the beginning of the year to teach your routines explicitly and practice them. Then revisit them throughout the year when students forget.

Use a checklist to help you keep up with your own classroom routines. Pilots use them. Nurses and doctors in emergency rooms use them. If you find yourself struggling to keep up with daily routine tasks, checklists work (see Gawande, 2010).

When I arrive at school each morning, the first thing I do is open my spreadsheet which lists the daily tasks I need to follow to keep myself on track. These are things like "check the staff calendar," "check daily announcements," and "set alarms for the day" (because our school doesn't use bells to mark the end and beginning of class, I set alarms on my phone as reminders). My list includes all the mundane tasks that I would otherwise forget to do. There is also a section for things I need to do at the end of the day: "mark student work," "straighten up desk," and "clear out email in-box."

I have added checkboxes beside each item – and it feels really good to check them off. My checklist even tells me how many "points" I get each day. If I hit 10 points (out of a possible 12), I give myself a reward. Fun! (It's easy to turn a spreadsheet into a checklist in Google Sheets or Excel – just look up how to do this on the web or YouTube.)

Clear communication about learning objectives. "Why are we doing this?" Students need to know the reason for the things you are asking them to do. If they perceive that the activity you have assigned is random or haphazard, or if they question the value of the activity, then they are less likely to engage. Instead, when you provide a clear goal for your students, they can concentrate their learning efforts on achieving that goal.

A simple way to be clear is to write the learning objective on the board. "At the end of today's lesson you will be able to solve a two-step algebra equation" or "Learning objective: Identify irony within a text and explain its purpose." Statements like these help students know what is important, what to attend to, and where to focus their energy. It also helps them self-assess at the end of the lesson – especially if you draw their attention back to the objective at the end of class.

However, writing the learning objective on the board is only one way to improve clarity – and it is not always necessary or appropriate. The fact is, learning experiences that we design for our students are multifaceted. Often, they are not meant to achieve one discrete objective – or even a few. Choosing one and writing it on the board may be helpful, or it may feel like you are oversimplifying a holistic process.

Sometimes all you need to do is to say "we are doing this (worksheet, exercise, repetitive practice) because it will prepare you for the next level." Or "this (activity, discussion, written assignment) will develop your ability to support your point with evidence." As objectives shift throughout the lesson, continue to draw your students (and your own) attention to the **why**.

You may have designed your lesson so that your students discover the learning objective for themselves – in which case, telling them up front would defeat the purpose. For example, an outdoor education class may involve participants in a group team-building challenge such as the Human Knot. Then, in reflection afterwards, students realize for themselves that the learning objectives were building trust, listening to peers, trying out different ideas, and so on. Telling them up front would erode this self-discovery process.

So, how you communicate learning objectives is context-dependent. The important thing is, students must have the sense that what they are doing is important. And equally important, ***you*** need to know what the learning objective is.

I observed a grade 8 science class where students were asked to model cell mitosis out of playdough. In the teacher's mind, the object was to acquaint students with the process of mitosis in a fun and creative way. In the students' minds, the object was to play with playdough. Very little learning happened that day; instead, students had a grand time messing about. If the teacher had been clear – both with herself and her students – about the lesson's objective (understanding cell mitosis), she might have delivered the information differently and set up the playdough task with clearer instructions: as a result, students might have been more focused on their learning.

Clarity around assessment. When you assign any work, test, or assignment, students need to know – ahead of time – how they will be assessed. This means you need to have developed the rubric or marking scheme beforehand.

In a points-based assessment, be clear how many points each section is worth. This gives students the ability to pace themselves and allocate their energy and time appropriately.

When assessment is qualitative (essays, performances, presentations, anything that assesses beyond right and wrong), share the grading rubric with students **before** they do the assignment. Ensure that the rubric clearly describes what quality looks like. Better yet, use exemplars to help students understand what quality looks like:

- Show students what a great presentation/essay/written response looks like – and what a not-so-great product looks like. Use exemplars from prior years' student work or create your own.
- Give your students three examples and ask them to decide which one is Proficient, which is Developing, which is Extending (or whatever grading language you use).
- Let your students mark the exemplars. Then discuss what led them to their grading decisions.
- Have students develop the rubric themselves, based on their reasons why this example is Proficient but that one is Developing.

The time that you spend getting organized is an investment – it will pay off in the long run. If you know that organization is your PPF, try the strategies above. Your life – and your students – will be much happier!

Further Reading

Chase, C. & Chase, J. (1997). *Tips from the trenches: America's best teachers describe effective classroom methods*. Although this book is a bit out of date, the chapter titled "Classroom Management" in both the elementary and secondary sections have excellent (non-digital) ideas for organizing your papers, systems etc. in order to keep your head above water.

Coursera course for getting organized: https://www.coursera.org/learn/together-teacher

Dueck, M. (2021). *Giving students a say: Smarter assessment practices to empower and engage*. ASCD. This is an excellent resource for creating clarity around assessment.

For organizing supplies and papers in elementary classrooms: *Teacher Organization Tips* in A Differentiated Classroom. https://adifferentiatedclass.com/teacher-organization/

Gawande, A. (2011). *The checklist manifesto: How to get things right.* Picador.

Harper, J., & O'Brien, K. (2015). *Classroom routines for real learning: Daily management exercises that empower and engage students.* Pembroke Publishers Limited.

Heyck-Merlin, M. (2021). *The together teacher: Plan ahead, get organized, and save time!* John Wiley & Sons.

Lemov, Doug. (2021). *Teach like a champion 3.0: 63 Techniques that put students on the path to college.* John Wiley & Sons. This is a superb resource for developing classroom routines.

PPF #6. Use Every Minute: Stop Wasting Time

Once I understood the importance of making every minute count – that is, how small increments of instructional time can add up to significant learning time lost or gained over the course of a year – I found that I was motivated to invest energy into using every minute in class. Sometimes just being aware of this impact can make all the difference.

The beginnings and end of the class are typically when the most time is lost. Try the following strategies:

- Have a "Do Now" written on the board. Teach your students to read the "Do Now" when they enter your classroom, and immediately get to work on the starter activity, rather than milling about waiting for class to start.
- Alternatively, set the expectation that when students enter the room, they are to sit at their desks and read silently until class begins – this requires that students always have reading material with them. Again, set this expectation at the beginning of the year. An acronym may help (e.g., "Always bring to class BAP: a book, your agenda, a pencil." Consider having a classroom library of appropriate reading material available for those who forget to bring their book.)

- Keep instructions concise, clear, and to the point. Train your students to listen to you the first time. Do not spend time repeating yourself. (See PPF #1.)
- Attendance: if you are required to take attendance at the beginning of the period, do so as efficiently as possible. Don't take the time to read through the roster, waiting for each student to say "here." Instead:
  - Count heads. Now you know that three students are missing. Ask the class to tell you which three are missing.
  - If your students sit in pre-assigned groups, ask students if anyone in their group is absent.
  - Use a seating plan – this way you will know at a glance who is not there.
  - Take a photo and mark the attendance after class is over. I did this for choir rehearsals when I had 80 to 100 students on my choir roster. You can then take attendance after the fact. (Students who arrived after the photo was taken would stay at the end of class for a special "late" photo.)
  - I know a teacher who does go through the attendance list student by student but uses that time as a personal check-in. "Olivia, how are you feeling today?" or "James, how's that new puppy of yours?" In this case, the time *is* well spent, as it is used to make personal connections.

The strategies for setting up routines described under PPF #5 (Get Organized) will help you use every minute of class time. Effective routines for recurring actions, such as passing out papers, collecting homework, handing back tests and assignments, and getting into groups will save you minutes every day. Compounded over (about) 180 teaching days, this adds up to significant instructional time. Remember: you must teach routines explicitly to students and practice them for them to work. Consistency matters.

Other ways to use class time efficiently for maximum learning:

- Tell students what they should do if they finish ahead of time, and make sure resources are available. For example, should they check their work, read the next chapter, buddy up with someone else who is finished and compare answers? Do you have reading material, a STEM (science, technology, engineering, and mathematics) bin, or a craft corner they can choose from?
- Attention-getters: Don't waste time waiting for students to stop talking. Train them to respond immediately to your signal when you need to gain their attention. Use attention-getters like "All eyes on me in 5 … 4 … 3 … 2 … 1." (See PPF #1 for more attention-getting strategies.)
- Be aware of how long your students are able to stay on task. If you plan a 15-minute group activity, but your students can sustain their focus on task for only 3 minutes before chatting off-topic, you risk wasting precious time. Keep an eye on how the groups are progressing, and be willing to move on or redirect if you notice your students becoming unproductive.
- We can't always predict how long a particular lesson or activity will last. So, always have a back-up plan or a repertoire of "sponge activities" available to "soak up" precious minutes that would otherwise be lost (Hunter, 2004). Examples of sponge activities are the following:
  - Highly engaging thinking tasks, such as the "good problems" on Peter Liljedahl's website Liljedahl (n.d.). For example, "How do you make a 9-minute egg if all you have is a 4-minute and 7-minute egg timer?"
  - Games like Four Corners (ModelTeaching, 2022). Label the corners of your classroom "strongly agree," "agree," "disagree," and "strongly disagree". Read a statement, give think time, then have students move to the corner that represents their response to the statement. The statement can relate to the lesson

content, current events, or other engaging topics. Once in their corner, students discuss the reasons for their choice with the others in the group and then choose a spokesperson to share with the class.

- With younger students, have a repertoire of class songs that you can sing together.
- Silent reading is always an effective use of time as long as students actually read and don't take the time to socialize. Keep a variety of reading materials in your classroom for these moments.

There are times when it is okay to relax and allow students to take time to "chill." As an educator responsible for social and emotional health as well as academic learning, you can, and should, make that call when it is in the best interest of the students. If they have just written a test or have experienced stress of one kind or another, the best use of time may **not** be to try to be productive. The important thing is to be **intentional** about your use of precious class time.

Further Reading

Fisher, D. & Frey, N. (2020) No instructional minute wasted. *ASCD*, 77(9). https://www.ascd.org/el/articles/no-instructional-minute-wasted

Harper, J., & O'Brien, K. (2015). *Classroom routines for real learning: Daily management exercises that empower and engage students*. Pembroke Publishers Limited.

Powell, A. (2009). *The cornerstone: Classroom management that makes teaching more effective, efficient, and enjoyable*. Due Season Press.

PPF #7. Set Boundaries: Students Need a Teacher, not a BFF

If your PPF is to shift from BFF mode to teacher mode, then self-awareness will be imperative. There is no doubt that your challenge with professional boundaries results from the fact that you care about your students. But there are better ways to be caring than trying to be overly close. When you are aware of this and of the impact your current approach has on students, you will be able to make the shift easily.

Encroaching on BFF territory has a significant negative effect on classroom management. When students perceive you as a buddy, your influence weakens. Consequences for poor behavior become personal. Students who think of you as a friend may become hurt or angry if you expect them to be accountable.

Additionally, every time a teacher develops a close bond with an individual student, other students perceive this and become resentful. A close bond with one or more students quickly creates a reputation as a teacher who "plays favorites." Students who are not "favorites" will assume you don't like them. Those who are "favorites" might assume the rules don't apply to them and will struggle to navigate the relationship.

Be aware of your role. You are not your students' friend, their parent, or their counsellor. You are a teacher – to all of your students. This requires professional distance so that you are in a position to influence their learning.

You can care ***that*** your students have a trusted adult, without trying to ***be*** that trusted adult yourself. If you find students sharing with you something that is beyond your role as teacher, listen empathetically, then encourage them to seek help from the appropriate source. Know your legal and ethical obligations for reporting disclosures related to child protection, such as self-harm or abuse.

The following list of guidelines comes from Michael Linsin's excellent website *Smart Classroom Management*:

- Be a teacher, mentor, and role model. Be friendly but never a friend.
- Maintain a polite, warm level of professional distance.
- Engage in the same friendly banter with all students.
- Don't use slang or popular terms with them.
- Model politeness and expect it in return.
- Follow your classroom management plan as it's written.

- Focus less on individual relationships and more on creating a classroom your students love coming to every day. (Linsin, 2011)

If, despite knowing all this, you recognize in yourself a deep need to be liked – in a peer-like manner – by your students, you may need to do some deeper work. Dr. Gabor Mate's work on attachment might be helpful (see "Further Reading," below). We are wired for attachment, and if our attachments needs are not met or were not met when we were children, it can put us at risk of seeking attachment in the wrong places. Don't impose your attachment needs on your students.

Worst-case scenario. Knowing your role, establishing teacher–student boundaries, and maintaining a professional tone are necessary protections against allegations of abuse. Don't blur the boundaries. Protect yourself.

Further Reading

Bernstein-Yamashiro, B., & Noam, G. G. (2013). Establishing and maintaining boundaries in teacher-student relationships. *New Directions for Youth Development, 2013*(137), 69–84.

Lahiri, A. (2021). *Elephant in the classroom: The essential teachers' guide to maintaining healthy boundaries with students*. ISBN 979-8595904582. https://www.amazon.ca/Elephant-Classroom-Essential-Maintaining-Boundaries-ebook/dp/B08T7Q9354

Maté, G. (2022). *The myth of normal: Trauma, illness, and healing in a toxic culture*. Penguin.

Stevens, G. (2023). *The ultimate boundaries playbook for teachers: Strategies and scripts to say no without guilt, ditch teacher tired, and create better work/life balance for educators*. Red Lotus Books.

PPF #8. Move the Bar: Set an Appropriate Level of Challenge

The student who is not challenged by the work you give them, or one who feels stressed because they do not have the tools, skills, or background knowledge to be successful, is a student whose needs are not met. Both will experience distress – boredom and apathy in the first case, anxiety and frustration in the second. Neither will be engaged and learning. The essence of good teaching is finding that sweet spot of instructional challenge (not too challenging, not too easy).

The place to start is pre-assessment. You must know where your students are before you can design appropriate instruction.

Pre-assessment simply means finding out, through the use of diagnostic testing, what the students already know and can do. Results from pre-assessment can inform your planning: there's no point teaching what students already know or designing activities that move too slowly when your students are capable of much more. On the other hand, assuming that students have prior knowledge that they don't actually have is equally problematic. It is no use thinking "they should have learned this last year." Maybe they learned it, maybe they didn't. You won't know without assessing their prior knowledge and capabilities.

You can pre-assess at the beginning of a unit by using a test similar to the end-of-unit summative test you intend to give. And here's a bonus: research shows that students learn more during the upcoming unit when they have been "primed" by writing a pre-test, even when they answer most of the questions incorrectly (Richland et al., 2009). Make sure your students understand the purpose for this pre-test (i.e., so that you will know how to design their upcoming learning experiences) and know that their scores on this pre-test will not enter the gradebook.

Other types of pre-assessment can include the following:

- A more relaxed Kahoot-type quiz;
- An assignment such as a writing diagnostic to assess written skills;
- Class discussion – although you may not get an accurate read on every student if they do not all participate;
- A KWL (Know, Want to know, Learned) chart (Ogle, 1986. See also Storm, 2023);
- Individual conversations with students;

- A self-assessment checklist where students rate their own abilities. (Can you add and subtract fractions such as ¾ – ½? Can you describe five ways that the invention of agriculture changed human societies?)

When you have a better understanding of what your students know, understand, and can do, you can design instruction that suits them. You will also be better equipped to differentiate their learning since students arrive in your class with a broad range of strengths, needs, and experiences.

Differentiation. Because students do not present as a homogeneous group, hitting the sweet spot for each of them of not too hard, not too easy will require differentiation. There are various approaches to differentiating learning experiences for students, including teaching to the middle, teaching up, Universal Design for Learning (UDL), and personalized learning.

Teaching to the middle. This is the most common approach to differentiation: design your instruction for students in "the middle," then (usually in time *after* class or in spare moments during class) provide add-ons for those who need more challenge and support for those who need more support.

The amazing Shelley Moore uses a bowling ball metaphor to illustrate the problems with teaching to the middle. In her hugely popular video (Moore, 2016), she explained that when you bowl, aiming at the middle of the pins typically produces a 7–10 split. That is, by aiming at the middle, you invariably leave one pin still standing on either side. (In Shelley's metaphor, the bowling ball is the lesson, the pins are the kids.) After we've taught our lesson, the ones left standing – the ones whose needs we haven't met – are the kids who need the most support and the kids who need the most challenge. Now, in bowling, you get two attempts per turn to knock down all ten pins. So because we get only one more chance to roll that ball (in school, we have limited time to provide extra support) we end up choosing one of the standing pins. The other is left standing – that is, we inevitably end up with kids whose needs aren't met. (Awesome metaphor, Shelley!)

UDL. Shelley, an advocate for UDL, says that professional bowlers never aim at the middle. In order to knock down the most pins, they aim at the pins that are the hardest to hit. In terms of education, this means teaching to the kids who need the most support – those with Down syndrome, with autism, with other needs. And it turns out, she says, the supports these kids need are the support that all the students need. Shelley advocates that teachers design instruction for those students who need the most support, and then layer on levels of challenge to accommodate the rest.

Teaching up. Carol Ann Tomlinson, on the other hand, advocates the "teaching up" approach. She argues that all learners benefit from being taught the way that "smart kids" are taught. When you "teach up," you plan your instruction to engage and challenge the most advanced learners while providing scaffolding that will allow all learners to achieve success (Tomlinson, 2021).

Both approaches differentiate instruction. Both require that you attend to students' needs – both for challenge and for supports. Either way, we have to put energy into adjusting the way we teach to meet everyone's needs.

Personalized learning. Advocates of personalized learning eschew the idea of aiming instructional level at any one group. Instead, personalizing learning gives every student an individualized program, with choices embedded so that they can capitalize on their strengths and meet their individual needs.

A classroom that fully embraces personalized learning might use classroom stations, where students rotate through different activities. For example:

- At an independent work station, students work at their own pace through PowerPoint presentations, curated videos, readings, and/or interactive learning programs on their personalized, digitized playlist.
- At a collaborative group station, students problem-solve together, work on a cooperative project, or engage in a peer-feedback session.
- At a teacher-led station, the teacher provides direct instruction to small ability-based groups.

Personalized learning typically relies on computer-assisted learning as a necessary ingredient for differentiation. While this can allow students to work at their own pace on a personalized program, there are disadvantages: adding more screen time to the students' days is one. Another is the belief that education should involve cooperation, communication, and collaboration with other humans, not computers. As Paul France said: "Personalization shouldn't be used to industrialize kids' learning; it should humanize it through dialogue, discourse, and inquiry" (France, 2021). Lots to consider here.

Provide choice. Provide dimensionality to your teaching by thinking about learning not as a vertical sequence of steps but as a broader exploration of concepts. All students learn the same concepts but are able to choose the depth and extent to which they engage. To illustrate, here are some examples:

- Beginning band class. Everyone has learned to play the same five notes. Students are encouraged to try to figure out how to play a song by ear, using those five notes. They can choose one of these, or they can invent their own song. This allows for an infinitely broad application of rhythms, note combinations, speed, expression, and dynamics.
- Grade 7 English Language Arts. We have been focusing on run-on sentences. I provide six examples of a run-on, ranging from fairly straightforward to long and extensive. Students are tasked with choosing one and re-writing it so that it is concise and precise. Students can add whatever details or additions that they wish to the rewritten text, providing opportunities for creative expression.
- Grade 11 Economic Theory. The summative assessment has a series of problems that range from basic to more complex, all addressing the same set of concepts. The questions are coded so that students know ahead of time which ones solved correctly will result in a grade of "Developing," which will result in a grade of "Proficient," and which ones are required for "Extending." Students can then choose the level of challenge they wish.

The more you can provide multiple levels for students to engage with the concepts you are teaching (and as long as the choices will stretch and accommodate all learners), the more you will be able to hit that "sweet spot."

Elicit and attend to feedback. If finding the appropriate instructional level is your challenge, then getting feedback from students while you teach them is crucial. Only they can tell you if they are struggling; only they can tell you if they are sufficiently challenged. How will you know?

- ♦ Read the room. Body language and comments from students will often convey whether or not you have hit the "Goldilocks" zone. Pay attention and respond.
- ♦ Use frequent formative assessment. The term "formative assessment" includes any method of assessing students' understanding that does not enter into the grade calculation. Checking for understanding (e.g., asking for a thumbs-up, thumbs-down, to show if students are with you) is a form of formative assessment. So is administering a test that you mark but do not include in the gradebook. The purpose of formative assessment is to give you feedback about your students' learning on an ongoing basis so that you can adjust your instruction to meet their needs.
- ♦ Talk to your students. Find a quiet moment to check in, one-on-one, about how they are finding the pace of your class. Is it challenging enough? Too challenging? These frequent check-ins may give you good information; however, keep in mind that some students will tell you what they think you want to hear, and some may not admit that they are struggling, in order to "save face."
- ♦ Elicit anonymous feedback from your students:
  - Use exit tickets asking students to indicate if today's lesson was "too hard, too easy, or just right."
  - Use Google Forms or a printed questionnaire with questions that ask about the level of challenge of various aspects of your teaching, from your presentations, to class discussions, to the written assignment, to the homework questions.
  - Keep an anonymous "suggestions" box in your room and invite students to use it to give you real and

honest feedback about the level of challenge they experience in your class. You can supply blank slips of paper or a mini-form with leading questions such as "What aspect of today's class was overly challenging for you?", "What did we do today that was a good challenge for you?", and "Do you feel like you need more challenge? What would that look like?"

Whether you need to increase the challenge, provide more supports, or both, we all need to abandon the "one size fits all" approach. Providing options and choices and being flexible, attentive, and responsive to student needs will go a long toward meeting your students where they are and engaging them in appropriately challenging learning activities.

Further Reading/Viewing

Fisher, D., & Frey, N. (2014). *Checking for understanding: Formative assessment techniques for your classroom*. ASCD.

Fletcher-Wood, H. (2018). *Responsive teaching: Cognitive science and formative assessment in practice*. Routledge.

Kalbfleisch, M. L., & Tomlinson, C. A. (1998). Teach me, teach my brain: A call for differentiated classrooms. *Educational Leadership*, *56*(3), 52–55.

Moore, S. (2016, April 4). *Shelley Moore: Transforming inclusive education* [Video]. YouTube. https://www.youtube.com/watch?v=RYtUIU8MjIYhttps://www.dawsoncollege.qc.ca/udl/news/bowling-as-an-udl-metaphor/

Tomlinson, C. A. (2021). *So each may soar: The principles and practices of learner-centered classrooms*. ASCD.

Tomlinson, C.A. (2023). *"Teaching up" to reach each learner (Quick reference guide)*. ASCD. https://www.ascd.org/books/teaching-up-to-reach-each-learner-quick-reference-guide?variant=QRG123035

Villa, R. A., & Thousand, J. S. (Eds.). (2005). *Creating an inclusive school*. ASCD.

PPF #9. Make It Safe to Make Mistakes: Create a Positive "Error Culture"

The research is clear: students' academic achievement is bolstered in classrooms with a positive error culture (e.g., Grassigner et al., 2018). And the error culture (positive or negative) results from the way the teacher handles errors in the classroom (Soncini et al. 2021). Simply put, it matters how you respond to student errors.

During instructional time, your students can – and do – observe all your responses to student contributions. So, your responses must consistently demonstrate that we learn from mistakes. Soncini et al. (2021) refer to positive teacher responses as "supportive error-handling strategies." Soncini's study documented six error-handling strategies that resulted in classrooms with a positive error culture:

1. Begin your lesson introduction with an explicit statement such as "You can learn from your mistakes, so it is important to try responding even if you are not sure about the right answer."
2. When starting whole-class discussion, use a cooperative, rather than competitive, invitation for student input, such as "Ok … Let's see if we will find the right answer together. Who would like to begin?"
3. Use wait time of at least 5 seconds to indicate that all respondents – not just the first hands up – are of value.
4. If the student's contribution is incorrect, celebrate it, and learn from it. Here are some possible ways to respond:
   - "I was hoping someone would say that, thank you! Let's talk about it."
   - "That is not exactly right, but, thanks to your answer, I realize that I may not have been clear. I'll try to clarify the question."
   - "Good try, I see where you're coming from. Now let's consider …"
   - "What makes you say that?" This invites the student to analyze their error.

- "Let's talk about how you came up with that answer, and what you can try next."

5. Immediately stop any negative reactions to the error from classmates, such as giggles or groans. Frame this around the idea that mistakes are more valuable than correct solutions, because they do more to help us understand than simply getting it right.
6. If the student's contribution is correct, do not praise. Instead, acknowledge the work or the thought process that went into the response. For example, rather than joyfully saying "Correct!" you could say: "I can see that you read the passage closely. What part of the text led you to that conclusion?"

What not to do:

- Advise students to answer only if they are certain their answer is correct.
- Ignore a student's mistake. If you call on one student and they answer incorrectly, do not simply switch to another topic without comment.
- Redirect the question to another student to correct the mistake made by the first pupil. This is called the "Bermuda triangle of error correction" (Oser & Spychiger, 2005).
- Simply saying "incorrect" or "wrong" in response to a wrong answer.
- Allow your facial expression to convey disappointment when a student answers incorrectly.

Other strategies you can pursue:

- Lead classroom discussions about errors that commonly occur. For example, ask your students to think of incorrect, but reasonable, responses to a question. Have them explain why their "mistake" is one that might easily trip others up.
- Consider shifting your approach from Direct Instruction (DI) to Productive Struggle (PS). Kapur and Bielaczyc

(2012) compared two groups of grade 7 math students: a DI group, where the teacher demonstrated the correct way to solve problems, and a PS group, where students collaboratively solved complex problems without any instructional support up until a teacher-led review. The PS group outperformed the DI group on subsequent tests because, the investigators believed, the PS group discovered how to learn from their errors rather than fear them. Teaching through PS is nuanced. The tasks must be challenging yet possible to solve given the students' skill level and experience. To explore this idea further, see Liljedhal's *Building Thinking Classrooms* (Liljedahl, 2020).

- "My Favorite No." This is a brilliant teaching strategy for building a positive error culture. The teacher chooses incorrect answers from student submissions and, with the class, explores in a very positive way why the response is incorrect, and why it is their "favorite." See the video at https://www.youtube.com/watch?v=uuDjke-p4Co (Maryland Formative Assessment, 2015).
- Acknowledge and respond to your **own** mistakes in a positive way. Model that making mistakes is part of learning. Thank students for pointing out your errors. "Yes, I see I forgot to carry the two. Thanks, Luca, I really appreciate your attention to details."
- The way you mark your students' work sends a message about errors, positively or negatively. Large red Xs or negative points scoring (marks off for infractions, such as calculation mistakes) sends the message that errors are bad. Instead, circle items that need to be corrected, or mark only the items that are correct. Allow students to correct their mistakes and redo work after receiving feedback.

Acknowledge mistakes and make their inherent value evident rather than ignoring or condemning them. A positive error culture helps students to learn from their mistakes, develop confidence in their abilities, and embrace challenge.

Further Reading

Dweck, C. S. (2006). *Mindset: The new psychology of success*. Random house.

Kapur, M., & Bielaczyc, K. (2012). Designing for productive failure. *Journal of the Learning Sciences*, *21*(1), 45–83.

Liljedahl, P. (2020). *Building thinking classrooms in mathematics, grades K-12: 14 teaching practices for enhancing learning*. Corwin press.

McMillan, J. H. (2017). *Using students' assessment mistakes and learning deficits to enhance motivation and learning*. Routledge.

PPF #10. Like Them All: Show Students You're on Their Side

What should you do if you discover that your students think you don't like them? Well, unfortunately, this is not going to be something you can solve with a "fake it till you make it" approach. Students can tell how you really feel about them. Your behavior, expressions, and words give it away, no matter how hard you try to mask your feelings. You are going to have to dig deep to shift your underlying attitude to one of unconditional positive regard (UPR).

The idea of UPR was developed by psychologist Carl Rogers for use in psychotherapy. UPR means being fully accepting and supportive of a person regardless of what they say or do. As teachers, it means making the choice to enjoy who our students are and to appreciate their unique personalities, without expectations. It challenges us to continually see the best in each of our students. And it means liking them, as people, despite what they say or do.

Dislike the behavior, not the person. We've all heard this maxim. However, sticking to it can be challenging with some of our students: the ones whose behaviors make our lives difficult, the students who say and do things we don't like, the students who take up our time and energy. This is where mindfulness comes in. Take the time to process your thinking about each of your "difficult" students. Notice the negative thoughts you may have. Be deliberate in separating the behavior from the person.

Adopt a curious mindset. Why is this student behaving the way they do? Yes, they may be acting out of a need for attention, but why do they need that attention? What, in their self-concept, in their home life, in their experience drives them to behave in ways that are inconvenient in a school setting? Ask yourself these questions and consider the possibilities. I am not suggesting that you take on the role of therapist – that is not your job. However, simply contemplating the possible reasons behind the behavior may shift your thinking from judging to questioning. And this can help soften your dislike of the person.

Frame behavior as choices rather than character. Our students are young. Their characters are forming. As they grow, they make choices to behave in one way or another. Sometimes, they make poor choices. Sometimes, they are choosing to use the only coping strategy they know. You can help them to learn to choose a better strategy. Teach behaviors, don't judge the person.

Praise praise praise. Make it your personal mission to praise every student, individually, every day (or on a regular basis if you have many students). Keep a chart and record your positive interactions with each child so that you know you are reaching them all, equally. This does take time and effort, but if this is your PPF, it's worth it. By actively working to find something to praise about each of your students, you will start to shift your mindset toward UPR.

A few caveats regarding praise:

- Praise the process, not the product. Not "Good painting," but "I like your choice of colors here."
- Praise the process, not the person. Not "You're a good artist," but "I notice you are really working hard to shade these corners." Praise determination and hard work, not natural ability.
- Be specific. Not "Good paper," but "I notice your first sentence was carefully crafted. Well done for taking the time!"
- Be authentic. "What you said in class today about the Big Bang was interesting. It really got me thinking."
- Don't praise students for doing what you expect them to do. If you have instructed them to push their chairs in at the end of class, do not praise them for doing so. Thank them instead.

Intentionally increase your positive-to-negative interaction ratio. Research shows that relationships thrive when the ratio of positive to negative interactions is at least 5 to 1 (Gottman & Gottman, 2017). If you find your communications with students are more often negative (scolding, correcting, reminding) than positive, work to shift this around. Set your intention to increase these kinds of interactions:

- Words of appreciation – for big and small things. "Thank you for your comment yesterday. It really helped your classmates understand the concept."
- Praise – see above.
- Humor – laugh at their jokes (when they are appropriate). It shows that you enjoy their company.
- Active listening – listen without interrupting or shifting the focus to yourself and without trying to "teach" something. Just listen. Listen to understand. Ask questions, summarize, and make eye contact.
- Words of validation – saying "That makes sense" or "I can understand why you feel that way" goes a long way to making students feel heard and understood.
- Friendly greetings – Greet them in a way that shows that they matter and that their presence is important. Slow down and really ask how they are doing. Then listen.

Pay particular attention to those students who seem to require constant corrections, reminders, and redirection, the ones who are harder to like. You will need to work extra hard on creating positive interactions with them in order to maintain a minimum 5-to-1 ratio.

Be aware of which student(s) you don't like. If you can be honest with yourself and admit to not liking one or some of your students, then start there. Work extra hard to find things to like about them. Take extra time to invest in positive interactions with them. Smile at them. If they give you attitude, don't take it personally. Their behavior is their choice – a bad choice, perhaps – but fundamentally, it has nothing to do with you. Make the decision to like them, no matter what.

Be aware of which student(s) you like more than others. Again, being honest with yourself and recognizing that you like some students more than others helps a lot here. If you know you like some students more than others, be extra careful to monitor your interactions with them. Know that perceived favoritism can result in resentment, anger, and bad morale in the classroom.

Of all the Professional Practice Focuses, PPF #10 ("Like them all: Show students you're on their side") is the most responsive to increased self-awareness. That is to say, if you know this is an issue for you, you'll be able to solve it by examining – and adjusting – your way of thinking. Journalling can help. And so can remembering that the students who are the hardest to like need our UPR most of all.

Further Reading

Flora, S. R. (2000). Praise's magic reinforcement ratio: Five to one gets the job done. *The Behavior Analyst Today*, *1*(4), 64.

Linsin, M. (2009). *Dream class: How to transform any group of students into the class you've always wanted*. Michael Linsin.

Pianta, R. C., & Allen, J. P. (2008). Building capacity for positive youth development in secondary school classrooms: Changing teachers'interactions with students In M. Shinn & H. Yoshikawa (Eds.), *Toward positive youth development: Transforming schools and community programs* (pp. 21–39). Oxford University Press. https://doi.org/10.1093/acprof:oso/9780195327892.003.0002

Venet, A. S. (2023). *Equity-centered trauma-informed education*. Routledge. See Chapter 7: Cultivate unconditional positive regard.

A Final Word

Professional growth is hard. It takes time and patience. Be kind to yourself. Be proud that you are investing time and energy to become a better teacher. Know that your students will benefit.

Notice the small wins and celebrate them. Engage in positive self-talk, like "I notice that I took the time this morning to listen to Ryan talk about his weekend soccer tournament – without interrupting him. Way to have an intentional positive interaction!" If you had access to an excellent instructional coach, this is the kind of language they would use. So be your own cheering squad, just like you are for your students.

References

Assor, A., Kaplan, H., Kanat-Maymon, Y., & Roth, G. (2005). Directly controlling teacher behaviors as predictors of poor motivation and engagement in girls and boys: The role of anger and anxiety. *Learning and Instruction*, *15*(5), 397–413.

Ben-Horin, O. (2016). Towards a professionalization of pedagogical improvisation in teacher education. *Cogent Education*, *3*(1), 1248186.

Berliner, D. C. (2008). The nature of expertise in teaching. In M. Cochran-Smith, S. Feiman-Nemser, D. J. McIntyre, & K. E. Demers (Eds.), *Handbook of research on teacher education* (3rd ed., pp. 808–823). Routledge.

Ferriss, T. (2017, May 15). Fear-setting: The most valuable exercise I do every month. *Blog of Tim Ferriss: Experiments in Lifestyle Design*. https://tim.blog/2017/05/15/fear-setting/

France, P. E. (2021, August 19). *Putting the person back in personalized learning*. ASCD 79(1). https://www.ascd.org/el/articles/putting-the-person-back-in-personalized-learning

Gawande, A. (2010). *Checklist manifesto: How to get things right*. Penguin Books India.

Gottman, J., & Gottman, J. (2017). The natural principles of love. *Journal of Family Theory & Review*, *9*(1), 7–26.

Grassinger, R., Scheunpflug, A., Zeinz, H., & Dresel, M. (2018). Smart is who makes lots of errors? The relevance of adaptive reactions to errors and a positive error climate for academic achievement. *High Ability Studies*, *29*(1), 37–49.

Gurland, S. T., & Evangelista, J. E. (2015). Teacher–student relationship quality as a function of children's expectancies. *Journal of Social and Personal Relationships, 32*(7), 879–904.

Hattie, J. (2023). *Visible learning: The sequel: A synthesis of over 2,100 meta-analyses relating to achievement*. Taylor & Francis.

Hunter, R. (2004). *Madeline Hunter's mastery teaching: Increasing instructional effectiveness in elementary and secondary schools*. Corwin.

Kapur, M., & Bielaczyc, K. (2012). Designing for productive failure. *Journal of the Learning Sciences, 21*(1), 45–83. https://doi.org/10.1080/10508406.2011.591717

Lemov, D. (2021). *Teach like a champion 3.0: 63 Techniques that put students on the path to college*. John Wiley & Sons.

Liljedahl. (n.d.). *Peter Liljedahl» Good problems*. https://www.peterliljedahl.com/teachers/good-problem

Liljedahl, P. (2020). *Building thinking classrooms in mathematics, grades K-12: 14 teaching practices for enhancing learning*. Corwin Press.

Linsin, M. (2009). *Dream class: How to transform any group of students into the class you've always wanted*. Michael Linsin.

Linsin, M. (2011, May 7). Why you should never, ever, be friends with your students. *Smart Classroom Management*. https://smartclassroommanagement.com/2011/05/07/never-be-friends-with-students

Linsin, M. (2022, February 11). Why a beautifully designed classroom is a bad idea. *Smart Classroom Management*. https://smartclassroommanagement.com/2022/02/11/beautifully-designed-classrooms

Maryland Formative Assessment. (2015, January 22). *Jan 21 Webinar video 1 (My Favorite No Video Slide 19)* [Video]. YouTube. https://www.youtube.com/watch?v=uuDjke-p4Co

McWhorter, J. (2019). Why grown-ups keep talking like little kids. *The Atlantic*. May, 2019.

Michaels, S., & O'Connor, C. (2015). Conceptualizing talk moves as tools: Professional development approaches for academically productive discussion. *Socializing intelligence through talk and dialogue* (pp. 347–362). American Educational Research Association.

ModelTeaching & Pond, S. (2022, May 11). *The four corners strategy-a verbal, active method to check for understanding*. Model Teaching.

https://www.modelteaching.com/education-articles/teaching-strategies/the-four-corners-strategy-a-verbal-active-method-to-check-for-understanding

Montuori, A. (2017). The complexity of improvisation and the improvisation of complexity: Social science, art and creativity. In S. Minahan (Ed.), *The aesthetic turn in management* (pp. 455–473). Routledge.

Moore, S. (2016, April 4). *Shelley Moore: Transforming Inclusive Education* [Video]. YouTube. https://www.youtube.com/watch?v=RYtUlU8MjlY

Ogle, D. M. (1986). KWL: A teaching model that develops active reading of expository text. *The Reading Teacher*, *39*(6), 564–570.

Oser, F., & Spychiger, M. (2005). *Lernen ist schmerzhaft: Zur Theorie des negativen Wissens und zur Praxis der Fehlerkultur*. Beltz.

Paulmann, S., & Weinstein, N. (2023). Teachers' motivational prosody: A pre-registered experimental test of children's reactions to tone of voice used by teachers. *British Journal of Educational Psychology*, *93*(2), 437–452.

Reeve, J., & Cheon, S. H. (2021). Autonomy-supportive teaching: Its malleability, benefits, and potential to improve educational practice. *Educational Psychologist*, *56*(1), 54–77.

Richland, L. E., Kornell, N., & Kao, L. S. (2009). The pretesting effect: Do unsuccessful retrieval attempts enhance learning? *Journal of Experimental Psychology: Applied*, *15*(3), 243.

Siacor, K. H., Ng, B., & Liu, W. C. (2023). Autonomy-supportive teaching on teacher social-emotional competencies. In B. Ng (Ed.), *Self-Determination Theory and Socioemotional Learning* (pp. 249–265). Springer Nature Singapore.

Soncini, A., Matteucci, M. C., & Butera, F. (2021). Error handling in the classroom: an experimental study of teachers' strategies to foster positive error climate. *European Journal of Psychology of Education*, *36*(3), 719–738.

Stichter, J. P., Stormont, M., & Lewis, T. J. (2009). Instructional practices and behavior during reading: A descriptive summary and comparison of practices in title one and non-title elementary schools. *Psychology in the Schools*, *46*(2), 172–183.

Storm, A. (2023, August 14). *KWL chart teaching & learning strategy: Examples, templates, and other strategies*. Thinkific. https://www.thinkific.com/blog/kwl-chart-teaching-learning-strategy/

Tomlinson, C. A. (2021). *So each may soar: The principles and practices of learner-centered classrooms*. ASCD.

Vansteenkiste, M., Aelterman, N., De Muynck, G. J., Haerens, L., Patall, E., & Reeve, J. (2018). Fostering personal meaning and self-relevance: A self-determination theory perspective on internalization. *The Journal of Experimental Education*, *86*(1), 30–49.

Vansteenkiste, M., Aelterman, N., Haerens, L., & Soenens, B. (2019). Seeking stability in stormy educational times: A need-based perspective on (de)motivating teaching grounded in self-determination theory. In E. N. Gonida & M. S. Lemos (Eds.), *Motivation in education at a time of global change: Theory, research, and implications for practice* (Vol. 20, pp. 53–80). Emerald.

Warren, P. (2016). *Uptalk: The phenomenon of rising intonation*. Cambridge University Press.

Wiggins, A. (2017). *The best class you never taught: How spider web discussion can turn students into learning leaders*. ASCD.

Wooden, J. (1973). *They call me coach* (p. 103). Bantam Books.

12

Conclusion

Teachers are drowning in advice. — Doug Lemov (2014)

When I set out to write this book, I didn't want to add to the endless supply of teacher improvement books out there. Because there are a lot – as Doug Lemov pointed out. You could read a new book about improving teaching every week for your entire career and never get through them all.

But I realized that we don't need them all. There are many things that we are already doing right. I don't want you to waste your time reading a book about scope and sequence if you are already succeeding at this aspect of your practice. Also, I don't want you investing in professional development sessions on Universal Design for Learning (UDL) or Understanding By Design (UBD) or Standards-Based Grading (SBG) – if you have a Blindspot that needs immediate attention.

People come to teaching with a tremendous variation of personality traits, preferences, styles, and experiences. Often, we'll default to teaching the way we were taught. Sometimes, we intentionally ***don't*** teach the way we were taught. (I had the world's most boring Economics 101 teacher – and I swore never to be like that.) You may already be doing – intuitively or intentionally – many of the things that teacher books out there are recommending. Or you may not. The question for you, as an

DOI: 10.4324/9781003490975-16

individual with all your quirks and charms, is: what is the most important aspect of your teaching that needs your energy and time right now? What is most getting in the way of being the teacher your students need?

I am hoping that this book has helped you figure this out. Because what I want for you is to develop the aspect of your teaching that will make the biggest difference in your classroom. I want you to feel empowered to make those changes that will really impact your students.

McKinsey & Company, the global consulting firm I referenced in the introduction, has produced new, post-pandemic research showing that nearly a third of US K-12 educators are thinking of leaving their jobs. Why? Compensation, unreasonable expectations, and an inability to protect their well-being were the primary reasons given. On the other hand, teachers willing to stay cite meaningful work as their chief motivator (Bryant et al., 2023).

I can't help you with compensation or unreasonable expectations. But I hope I can help you to find your work more meaningful through becoming a better teacher. The more effective and impactful our teaching, the more success we will see students having in our classroom, and the more rewarding we will find the teaching profession. We owe it to ourselves to invest in our own professional growth by developing our self awareness and figuring out where to dig for our own personal professional development gold.

How well we teach the next generation of humans matters. Tomorrow's adults are in our hands: there is no more important job. This means that what we do to level up our game matters not just for us, for our school, or even our students but for all the people that our students will interact with, work for, lead, parent, and teach in the future. Whether you are a new teacher, a struggling teacher, or a teacher with years of experience behind you, I invite you to join me in the commitment to continuous improvement. One Blindspot at a time.

References

Bryant, J., Ram, S., Scott, D., & Williams, C. (2023, March 2). *K–12 teachers are quitting. What would make them stay?* McKinsey & Company. https://www.mckinsey.com/industries/education/our-insights/k--12-teachers-are-quitting-what-would-make-them-stay

Lemov, D. (2014, July 30). *On teachers and the advice they get*. Teach Like a Champion. https://teachlikeachampion.org/blog/teachers-advice-get/

Appendices

Appendix A

Tools to Support Classroom Discussion

Sentence Starters for Middle and High School

Adapted from various, including Avci (2020), Encouraging (2018), and K.D. (2023).

Agreeing

- "I feel the same way as *Jamal*, because…"
- "I like what *Sophie* said because…"
- "I agree with *Amin*; another example that confirms this is…"
- "I concur with *Dominique* about X, but for a different reason…"
- "Now that I have heard *Alexander*'s point of view, I'm rethinking my idea that…"

Disagreeing

- "I disagree with *Madeline* because…"
- "My thinking differs from *Ben's* because…"
- "I can see that X; however, I disagree with *Zachary* about Y because…"

Clarifying

- "*Liam*, Could you please repeat that for me?"
- "*Lukas*, Could you explain a bit more, please?"
- "*Clare*, I'm not sure I understood you when you said X.
- "*Elliott*, could you say more about that?"
- "What's your evidence to support that statement, *Olivia*?"

Paraphrasing

- "So you are saying that…"
- "What I hear *Jake* saying is…"
- "In other words…"

Extension

- "To add on to *Noah's* idea…"
- "To expand on what *Alyssa* said…"

Exploring possibilities

- "This makes me think…"
- "I want to know more about…"
- "I wonder…"
- "Is it possible that…"

Sentence Starters for Elementary School

Adapted from various, including Avci (2020), Chapin et al. (2009), and K.D. (2023).

Asking a question

- "What did you mean when you said…?"
- "Why do you think that way?"

Expressing an opinion

- "In my opinion… "
- "It seems to me that…"

Agreeing

- "I agree with *Kaylee*, because… "
- "That is a good idea, because…"

Disagreeing

- "I see it differently than *Sophie*, because…"
- "I disagree with *Aiden*, because…"

Making a connection

- "This reminds me of…"
- "This is like…, but different, because…"

References

Avcı, Ü. (2020). Examining the role of sentence openers, role assignment scaffolds and self-determination in collaborative knowledge building. *Educational Technology Research and Development*, *68*(1), 109–135.

Chapin, S. H., O'Connor, M. C., & Anderson, N. C. (2009). *Classroom discussions: Using math talk to help students learn, Grades K-6*. Math Solutions.

Encouraging academic conversations with talk moves. (2018, November 16). *Edutopia*. https://www.edutopia.org/video/encouraging-academic-conversations-talk-moves

K.D. (2023, September 5). *Inspires young minds with talk moves strategies*. The Teach Simple Blog. https://teachsimple.com/blog/teaching-strategies/talk-moves/

Appendix B

Talk Moves for Teachers to Support Student Voice

To support student talk in the classroom, research-backed "talk moves" for teachers are effective tools for supporting robust learning. Adapted from O'Connor and Michaels (2019) and Park et al. (2017)

1. To help students verbalize and share their thoughts:
   - **Wait time: Give time for students to think before responding.**
   - **Writing as thinking: Give students the opportunity to write their ideas down before sharing them verbally.**
   - **Partner talk: Allow students to voice their ideas peer to peer, before having them share with the entire class.**
2. To encourage students to clarify, expand, and elaborate on their thinking:
   - **"Interesting. Go on."**
   - **"Can you say more about that?"**
   - **"Why do you think so?"**
   - **"Can you give an example?"**
   - **"Let me see what you are saying. Are you saying…?" (Then give the student time to clarify and elaborate.)**
3. To elicit evidence or reasoning:
   - **"Why do you think that?"**
   - **"What's your evidence?"**
   - **"How did you arrive at that conclusion?"**
   - **"Is there anything in the text that made you think that?"**

4. To deepen student thinking:
    - **"How does that square with Austin's idea?"**
    - **"Does it always work that way?"**
    - **"What if it had been raining that day instead?"**
5. To support students in orienting to others and listening carefully:
    - **"Who can put what Sophie said in your own words?"**
    - **(After partner talk) "What did your partner say about…"**
6. To encourage students to engage in others' thinking:
    - **"What do you think about what Javon said?"**
    - **"Do you agree or disagree with Lena, and why?"**
    - **"Does anyone want to respond to that idea?"**
    - **"Can anyone take Jada's suggestion and push it a little further?"**
    - **"Who can explain what Namir meant when he said…?"**

References

O'Connor, C., & Michaels, S. (2019). Supporting teachers in taking up productive talk moves: The long road to professional learning at scale. *International Journal of Educational Research*, *97*, 166–175.

Park, J., Michaels, S., Affolter, R., & O'Connor, C. (2017). Traditions, research, and practice supporting academically productive classroom discourse. In *Oxford research encyclopedia of education*. Oxford University Press.

Appendix C

The Classic Ten for Use in Forced Choice

For use during the Forced Choice exercise (Chapter 6). Give this list to your colleague to use, along with the guidelines below.

1. Cut the words – Reduce teacher talk, increase student talk.
2. Fix verbal hazards – Check habits like shrillness, lack of presence, repetitive phrases, baby voice, monotone, or upspeak. (You can indicate which of these apply.)
3. Loosen the reins – Stop micromanaging – students are more capable and need more agency.
4. Dial back overpreparation – Be more responsive to student needs.
5. Get organized – Provide students with clarity, consistency, and accountability.
6. Use every minute – Stop wasting time.
7. Set boundaries – Students need a teacher, not a BFF.
8. Move the bar – Set an appropriate level of challenge (you can tell me if I'm aiming too high, too low, or both).
9. Make it safe to make mistakes – Create a positive "error culture."
10. Like them all – Show students you're on their side.

Please consider my practice and choose the one item from the list above that you feel I should prioritize.

- If you feel more than one applies, choose the one that will have the biggest impact on my teaching and my students' learning.
- If you feel none applies, please still choose one.
- Don't tell me how *much* it applies – just tell me the one.

These guidelines are meant to protect my ego and yours!